Money Secrets

for the

Sandwich Generation

(Squeezed in the Financial Middle)

By

Patricia A. Davis

Money Secrets

for the

Sandwich Generation

(Squeezed in the Financial Middle)

Copyright © 2014 by Patricia A. Davis

Published by Davis Financial Services

ISBN 978-0-9827037-2-4

Library of Congress cataloging in—Publication Data

Money Secrets for the Sandwich Generation

(*Squeezed in the Financial Middle*) / Patricia A. Davis

Money Secrets for the Sandwich Generation presents general financial information and guidance for those who are members of the sandwich generation now or expect to be in the near future. The author is not rendering specific legal or financial advice. If such assistance is needed, readers should seek the guidance of qualified legal or financial advisors.

Printed in the United States of America

DEDICATION

*To those of you who are caring for both aging parents and adult or minor children while still trying to take care of yourselves, you are members of the **Sandwich Generation**!*

I hope within these pages, you will find the information needed to help make the challenges a little easier and the wisdom and courage to use it. I only ask that you pay it forward.

ACKNOWLEDGMENTS

As soon as my first book, *Mimi, Money and Me*, came out, I was encouraged by many who read it to write a second one. For a while, I resisted. As I continued my financial literacy teaching and counseling, I came to realize there was a group of people struggling to find their financial (and emotional) balance as they dealt with similar stressful situations for which they needed assistance and direction. It is because of their willingness to open their lives and share their stories that I took this incredible journey to understand their challenges, to look for solutions, and to become knowledgeable enough to share some of what I have learned with you. So, to the participants in my workshops, to my clients, and to those I've met along the way, I want to say a heartfelt thank you.

In addition to those who were so candid with me, there are many others who helped make this new book possible.

Of course this whole journey began with my Mother who laid the foundation of financial knowledge for her children. Thank you, Mimi, for setting the stage for me to learn and comprehend the rules of the money game. You promised your lessons would "last a lifetime," and, they have. Now, I'm trying to "pay it forward."

Thank you to my husband, Jim Davis, for your love, support and confidence, and for believing I have a message worth "sharing." You read the early drafts; painstakingly took the time to make comments on virtually every page; and gently prodded me to continue even when I wanted to stop. Your faith in me never wavered and you have been an invaluable, critical resource that I never could have done without. You are the wind beneath my wings.

Thank you to my sisters, Beverly Tobias, Janet Briggs and Denise (Nisey) Coleman who gave me some of the answers when I asked them, "What would Mimi say?" about specific challenges of the sandwich generation. We all agreed on how she would have directed and encouraged each of us that we can "fight the fight and win the war." She also would have reminded us that "He never gives you more than you can handle."

Thank you to Annette Ferrell, Kathy Henschel, Ken Marsala and Lee Straus whose comments on the pre-edition drafts helped expand my thinking; made my chapters more realistic and compassionate; and taught me a few things I may not have realized about what is real today for this new generation. Each of you helped make this a better product.

Thanks to Jackie Byrd, the elder care attorney who wrote most of the chapter on "Long-term Care Giving." Her years of dealing with legal issues for seniors and her experience in writing the weekly "Senior Moments" column for the *Bowie Blade-News*, combined to make her the perfect resource for this topic.

Thanks to Michelle Singletary, the author of the *Washington Post's* syndicated bi-weekly column, the "Color of Money," who once interviewed Mimi for her annual "Penny Pinchers" contest. You wrote so positively about **Mimi, Money and Me** and have opened the eyes of many to the need to get control of their own financial future. And, you have made it easier for many of us who teach this extremely important subject to find a more open, more willing and more informed listening audience.

Thank you to Margaret E. Steele, my editor, whose tough, eagle-eyed style made the book an easier, more understandable read for all of you.

Thank you to DeBrosia Griffin, my virtual assistant, who so tirelessly formatted each chapter, and gave the book a more eye-appealing layout. Your tenacity and professionalism exceeded my wildest expectations.

Finally, thank you to my network of friends and colleagues whose encouragement has allowed me, once again, to serve as a platform for those who may not feel they have a voice.

Here's the book many of you asked for. Hope you enjoy the read!

TABLE of CONTENTS

TABLE of CONTENTS

The Story Behind This Book

Before telling you how this book came about, I would like to thank those of you who helped make my first book, *Mimi, Money and Me - 101 Realities About Money Daddy Never Taught Me but Mama Always Knew*, so successful. You bought it for yourselves; you gave it as gifts to family and friends; and you read it. Many of you incorporated several of the ideas and suggestions in it and have gone on to live healthier and wealthier lifestyles. (*Mimi, Money and Me* is available on my website *www.yourmoneywiz.com*, Amazon, BarnesandNoble.com, and the iBookstore.)

A number of you told me you fell in love with my Mother, Mimi, the matriarch who started it all for her offspring by insisting that we play the money game according to her very strict rules. She was tough, but my siblings, my readers, my clients and I have gained knowledge from her wise counsel and no-nonsense approach to money management. Each of us is all the better for it. Thanks, again, Mimi!

Most people did not have the benefit my siblings and I had of having a parent who taught them even the basic rules of the game of money. After many years of experience in the world of **corporate** finance, I realized that my true passion really is in the area of **personal** finance and helping others improve their lives by giving them the information they need to make better financial decisions for themselves, their families and their communities. With my mission very clear to me, I left corporate America and set out to follow my calling - to teach and to reach as many people as possible and spread the word regarding the who, what, when, where and why of the money game, and how to play it to win. I became a "financial education zealot," talking to anyone who would listen.

As I have continued teaching classes, counseling everyday folks and listening to my friends' and colleagues' stories about some of the challenges they themselves are dealing with, it has become clear to me that the financial elements of people's lives are changing from the way they used to be "back in the day." There seems to be a familiar theme in their stories. Many are about the pressures - financial and otherwise - they feel as they try to take care of their own needs while, at the same time, helping to care for a whole host of others. If you are simultaneously caring for aging parents while supporting your own offspring, be they minors or adults, welcome to the new **sandwich generation**!

In many cases, sandwich generation-ers say they feel like they're sitting on a three-legged stool that's a bit wobbly and they're trying not to fall off. Some say they're frustrated, perplexed and just plain exhausted as they try to figure out the next best courses of action to take. In other words, they feel "squeezed" and can't seem to catch their breath.

So, why did I write the book? I wrote it to 1) describe who this group is and how it came to be; 2) help clarify what some of issues are; 3) provide you with a list of available resources to help lighten your load; and 4) offer some tried and true recommendations about ways to manage yourself successfully through many of the situations you will recognize as being only too familiar and, oh, so confusing.

I have been teaching financial literacy and counseling clients for a long time and have seen, first hand, the impact making even small changes in the way you approach life situations can have. Given that experience, I wanted to share some of what I've learned to keep you from having to walk this journey alone without answers to the many questions you may have.

Although my spouse and I have no children, we are members of a close knit family that has dealt with many of the issues faced by members of the sandwich generation. As Mimi needed more care, her children and extended family banded together, developed a strategy that made the situation workable, and each did our part. So, I know from experience that you can come out with all three legs of the stool firmly planted.

Know that by your own actions, you have the power within you to erase the guilt, bewilderment and sense of helplessness you might feel if you are a member of the sandwich generation (or even know somebody who is). Knowledge is power! You just need a bit of ammunition to fight the fight. Hopefully, this book will ignite the flame and provide some of what you need to succeed.

Patricia

I. Historical Perspective and Profile

of the

Sandwich Generation

Who you are…

Where you are…

What you look like…

What your responsibilities are…

Historical Perspective and Profile

of the

Sandwich Generation

As mentioned earlier, the term **sandwich generation** refers to those people (mostly middle-aged) who are simultaneously supporting aging parents, and their own growing or grown children and grandchildren. Most are likely working a full-time job, also. The non-profit Pew Research Center says that more than 1 in 8 Americans are middle-aged sandwich generation-ers. The members of this generation are not centrally located. They are spread rather evenly across the nation.

A recent American Association of Retired People (AARP) survey showed that 35% of baby boomers (those born between 1946 and 1964) have, at some point, been responsible for caring for an elderly parent. At the same time, half are either raising a young child or are helping an adult child. All of these respondents are members of the sandwich generation.

What's behind all of this and where is it heading? This "aging of America" trend is expected to continue or get worse. The U.S. Census Bureau projects that, by 2030, the number of Americans 65 or older will represent about 20% of the U.S. population, up from 12.5% in 2000. It also projects the percentage of the population 85 and older will grow from 1.5% in 2000 to 2.3% by 2030—a 53% increase! According to the *Journal of Financial Service Professionals*, " ... at the start of the 20th century, only 4-6% of people in their 60s had at least one parent still living. Today, that figure is almost 50%!" Here are a few cases of longevity:

- My 80-year old neighbor's Mother has an identical twin sister who is now 104 years old and is still going strong. (His own Mother lived to the ripe old age of 101.) Her son is a politician and she continues to hit the campaign trail with him.

- A 75 year old colleague's Father is 93 years old. His wife, her Stepmother, is 102.

- The local newspaper recently carried a story about a group of four male friends who, for years, have meet each weekday morning to exercise together at the mall. The youngest one in the group is 91.

Baby boomers were mid-career when the retirement landscape shifted from regular defined benefit pension plans, as their parents had known them (where the pension amount is based on one's salary and years of service), to 401(k) and similar plans. Also, many were hit hard during the 2007-2009 recession and may not have fully recovered financially before retirement. As a result, according to the Transamerica Center for Retirement Studies' 2014 survey results, more than half of baby boomers expect to continue working in retirement, mainly to provide income and health benefits. A whopping 65% plan to work past age 65 or don't plan to retire at all.

As more and more baby boomers enter the sandwich generation category, the need to understand the dynamics of aging and family relationships becomes increasingly important. Several national, previously unheard of demographic trends combine to create this new sandwich generation. Until recently, the need to at least partially support aging parents and adult children simply didn't exist, and most people in their 50s and 60s weren't part of a sandwich generation. The role reversal where the baby boomer assumes the role of parent – either financially or emotionally - and the parent takes on the role of having their "child" assume responsibility for most of the parent's major decisions, is certainly a new dynamic and is a blow few may have seen coming.

The Mother of a long-time friend who is an only child, began experiencing signs of dementia. The 3,000 mile distance between them complicated her ability to closely monitor her Mom and to ensure her safety. After the disease progressed, for about a year, she and her retired husband relocated to where Mom lived. At some point, they made the decision to return home and to bring Mom with them. Two years later, Mom's isolation and loneliness caused them to re-visit their decision and they eventually took her back to her hometown to more familiar (at times) surroundings and placed her in a nursing home. It was a difficult decision laced with feelings of guilt and sadness. They go back to visit with her periodically and check on her regularly. At the same time, they are dealing with an adult child with a malady too serious for him to work; so, they cover all of his expenses. They are a classic case of a couple being "squeezed" both financially and emotionally.

In another case, both parents of a colleague, the devoted Father of two young girls, have been seriously ill. Though his Mother is recovering nicely, his Father's health is in serious decline. This colleague regularly adjusts his work schedule to have the flexibility needed to help care for his parents, who live about 75 miles from where he lives and works. He schedules and takes his Dad to medical appointments, oversees his care, and spends a couple of nights a week at his parents' home. Meanwhile, his daughters' school and extra-curricular activities keep him busy on the other side. In many ways, he is "Fathering" two generations – both his parents and his young children.

Several factors make it likely that this trend will continue for some time to come, at least as it relates to helping the older generation.

1.   With medical advances, people are living longer than in the past, leading to "the graying of America." This makes it more likely that your parents will need help as they age.

2.   Pensions of old - where you get a generous percentage of your salary based on years of service - are disappearing, causing a strain on seniors' ability to financially take care of themselves. Thus, often for economic reasons, multi-generational American families live together in greater numbers than ever before.

3.   The divorce rates for couples older than 50 has doubled in the past 20 years, reports the National Center for Family and Marriage. Many of these divorcees, now alone, say they have no plans to remarry. Thus, they forego the cheapest caregiver they'd ever find - a spouse. In many instances, they then turn to their adult children for help.

4.   The percentage of multi-generational households in the U.S. has increased 32.2% since 1980 - from 12.0% to 16.1% in 2010. The U.S. Census Bureau projects it will increase to 19.0% by 2030, mostly for economic reasons.

According to the AARP 2013 Career Study on Older Workers (ages 45-74), " ... 58% say they are responsible for caring for

someone they know such as a parent, child, spouse or friend. ...
Many of these adults today find they need to continue to work in
order to help family members financially while others need
flexibility in their work schedules to meet care-giving demands.
Some find that they need to cut back on their hours or retire
prematurely in order to provide care-giving."

Helping your parents or in-laws is only half of the story. On the
other side of the "big squeeze" we have young adults relying on
their parents for financial help. As recently as 1990, only about
25% of young adults 18-24 lived with their parents. A mere 10
years later, by 2000, the number had grown to 52% and continues
to rise. This trend is pushing older adults into the sandwich
generation with them having to provide assistance to both adult
children and to their own parents. A review of several economic
indicators helps explain why this trend started several years ago.

1. There are those who delayed parenthood and have younger
    children at home with many still facing the financial
    uncertainty of college expenses. So, many of their children
    are getting ready to go to college, are in college, or may
    return home once or twice after college or between jobs in
    an effort to "get on their feet." In any event, much of the
    financial responsibility still lies with the parents.

2. The economic recovery has been somewhat lackluster and
    many adults are unable to find jobs that pay enough so they
    can be self-supporting. As a consequence, many have
    moved back home with their parents. They are referred to
    as the "boomerang" generation - they leave but come back.
    Rising housing prices; high interest rates; and few financial
    reserves point to adult children crying out for **HELP**.
    Parents often answer the call which can, in and of itself, put
    a squeeze on them and hamper any efforts to get their own

financial houses in order. (Mimi said, "Every goodbye is not gone. They sometimes come back.")

3. Once children reach adulthood, many increasingly face hefty college debt and likely need financial assistance from their parents (at least temporarily) either to help with their loan payments or, in many cases, make the payments for them, especially if the parent was a co-signer.

> *Consider a recent 40-year-old client who has a relatively new PhD. She has more than $250,000 in student loans! When we met, her deferment period was about to end; so, she will soon have to start making payments on those loans. She has no parents to fall back on. Unless she gets involved in some sort of debt reduction or loan forgiveness program, she is not likely to pay off those loans in her lifetime. (See Chapter IV for a discussion of these types of programs.)*

What is the end result of all of this? It looks like the sandwich generation will be "squeezed" in the middle for some time to come.

Don't despair. All hope is not lost. While being part of the sandwich generation and caring for others can be hard on your physical and emotional health, as well as on your financial well-being, there are steps you can take to help smooth your ride. To learn what some of them are and how to make sure you're looking after yourself while caring for others, keep reading. In the next chapter, Taking Care of Yourself First, we'll discuss many of them.

II. TAKING CARE of YOURSELF FIRST

(Making sure you're OK)

What Would Mimi Say

about

Taking Care of Yourself First?

❖ *Self-preservation is the first law of nature.*

❖ *Save some for a rainy day.*

❖ *God grant me the serenity to accept the things I cannot change, the courage to change the things I can and the wisdom to know the difference.* (Regarding doing the best you can in any situation)

❖ *You can't spend it but once.*

Taking Care

of

Yourself First

Let's talk about YOU! While you may have spent a lifetime of putting others' needs ahead of your own, as a member of the sandwich generation, it's time to make an exception to that rule. It's time to start taking care of your own needs, first.

When the flight attendant broadcasts the emergency procedures, what instructions are you given? Aren't you told, " … in the event of an emergency, put your mask on first"? Yes, you are. In other words, you cannot take care of someone else who may need help if you haven't taken care of yourself. No, you are not being selfish at all. The reality is quite the contrary. In doing so, you are merely trying to make sure you are the best parent, child, caregiver, etc., that you can possibly be. And, you can't do that unless you have your own house in order.

As a member of the sandwich generation, there are all kinds of things you have to think about, make careful choices about, learn about and implement. Some are legal; some are medical; some are emotional; and some are financial. Each of these categories applies to you, your parents and your children (both adults and minors).

The strain on you and the financial burdens that come with caring for multiple generations can be both staggering and overwhelming and can negatively impact your own household's well-being. For purposes of this discussion, we will focus primarily on the financial matters you need to pay careful attention to and offer some tips to help smooth your path and lighten your load as you travel down this road.

From a financial perspective, there will be tugs at you from all sides - your own financial needs and wishes, those of your offspring, and those of your parents. You will need to understand the ramifications of each set of needs and wants, and proceed carefully. So, let's examine some of the things you need to do to help ensure your own financial well-being.

Commit to getting your own finances in order!

One of the first things you must do is develop an understanding of any of the needs of your parents and children that may have an impact on your financial resources. Armed with information gleaned from discussions with them, make a commitment to assess your family's financial situation to determine the extent to which you can help without jeopardizing your financial well-being. Then, move to straighten out your own finances.

To do so, develop a **budget** for yourself that crosses generational lines. This is the only way to be sure you have set a realistic expenditure plan that can be supported by the level of your resources. If followed strictly, it will help guide you in such a way that "your income will not exceed your outgo and your upkeep will not be your downfall." In other words, it will help you live within (or below) your means.

You have to learn to manage your money wisely to be able to live on the resources available to you. If you don't, you will probably have money problems. Careful planning will help you live within the confines of the resources you actually have. Mimi would have reminded you, 1) "You can't spend it but once!" and 2) "Money doesn't grow on trees!"

For those of you who have read my earlier book, **Mimi, Money and Me - 101 Realities About Money Daddy Never Taught Me but Mama Always Knew,** some of the budgeting information will be a refresher. For those who haven't, the discussion below is a jumping-off point to get those of you "squeezed in the financial middle" thinking about and preparing for some of the many issues you either are facing now or await you down the road.

First, let's define what a budget is and what it is not. By definition, a budget is a step-by-step plan for meeting your expenses during a specified period - usually 6- to 12 months. It is not a straight jacket. It is not a stationary guide to be set up once and never revised even when there has been a significant change in your life circumstances. Rather than being restrictive, as some people think, its intent is to help you make smart money decisions and provide an at-a-glance view of where you may have flexibility in your spending. Once you've created it and are comfortable that it captures the essential elements of your financial life, a budget can be one of the most liberating guides you've ever used. If done properly and followed, you know you can meet the obligations included without much thought and without any worry. Then, you are free to focus on other important elements of your life.

Budgeting is not a solo activity. Rather, it should be put together with input from family members about their expense needs and wants. That way, everybody is aware of what's in it and what you can and cannot afford to do.

In my own household, as you might have guessed, I take the lead in putting together our annual budget. (There are just the two of us.) We start in late fall talking about major things we want to do in the next year, such as savings amounts, new financial obligations, vacations, house projects, big celebrations, major purchases, gifts, charitable donations, etc. We then decide on an amount we want to allocate to each. If there are any changes on the income side, they get factored in, as well. I run the numbers and make sure the resources listed can support the expenditure pattern laid out. If they don't, then we make the necessary expenditure cuts until the budget balances.

During the next month or so, we make additions and subtractions if priorities change or we realize anything has been left out. By January 1st, we usually have things pretty well tied down. We don't finalize the budget until after the new year's first (and sometimes second) paycheck(s), since it isn't until then that we know the exact amount of the net paychecks, given all the new deductions. After that, it's done! We both know we can do the things listed and don't have to worry about whether we can afford something, as long as we stay within the income and expenses shown in the budget. Because we have been doing this for so long, there are rarely surprises. The timing is sometimes a little off and actual amounts may differ slightly from what is in the budget. But, all in all, it sets us free to operate pretty much on auto-pilot without having to worry.

When you construct your budget, it should include every dollar of income you expect to get during the time period covered, as well as every category of expense you expect to incur. For example, if you are supporting minor children, back-to-school clothes, Christmas gifts, class trips and the like are expenses you are certain to incur. If you own a car, at some point, there will be auto-related expenses like repairs, license renewal, gas, and insurance, so they all should be included in your budget. If you're a homeowner, expect that sometime over the next 6 to 12 months, something in your house will break down and will need to be serviced or replaced. You may not know the exact timing or dollar amount the repair or replacement will cost, but some amount should be shown in the budget. If you have close family members and you usually give birthday gifts, an amount should be reflected in your budget in the actual months they occur.

Mimi lived to be 83 years old. In every one of those 83 years, she had a birthday on August 29th and I'd better have her present! She didn't go without having a birthday some years and never had more than one birthday in any year. Our budget has a line item for birthday gifts and, you'd better bet, as long as she was alive, there was an entry in August.

For some reason, people often hesitate to include many of the above types of costs under the misguided assumption that not writing them down means they won't be incurred. That kind of thinking is unrealistic and you will end up having a budget that doesn't reflect your real income or expenses and one that could lead to you being unable to meet unbudgeted expenses when they arise.

Although, initially, exact dollar amounts for various types of expenditures may be only a "best guess estimate," experience and careful recordkeeping eventually lead to more accurate numbers. (See Appendix A for a detailed discussion of how to create a budget and for an example of one for a typical sandwich generation family with both spouses working.) You can go to my website at *www.yourmoneywiz.com* and download the electronic version.

Income sources might include:

- Net salaries from regular job
- Net income from part-time job/side jobs
- Disbursements from retirement plans
- Bonuses

- Social Security income
- Tax refunds (federal and state)
- Interest and dividends
- Alimony
- Child support
- Gifts

In other words, every dollar of income you expect to get should be listed in the "Resources" section of your budget.

In the "Expenses" section, you should include things like:

- **Regular Savings** - even if the amount is miniscule. Always try to put something away for unplanned expenses. (Mimi said, "Always save some for a rainy day.")
- **Retirement Savings in a tax-deferred 401(k), 403(b), or TSP (the federal government's equivalent of a 401(k)),** at least up to the level of the employer match, if you are still working and there is a match. You must begin to do retirement planning that incorporates the new reality of your expanded, multi-generational responsibilities. The result of such planning could indicate that life in retirement may not be as robust or exotic as you had initially planned. Nonetheless, you must calculate the dollars that you'll need to support whatever lifestyle you hope to maintain. Don't sabotage your own retirement by cutting out or back on this critical expense!
- **Donations/Tithing** - at whatever level represents your commitment and what you can comfortably afford
- **Mortgage/Rent Payments** - depending upon whether you are a homeowner or a renter
- **Condo/HOA fees** - if you have to pay them
- **Taxes – federal and state**
- **Home Repairs** - if you are a homeowner
- **Utilities** - including water, gas/electric, home phone, cell phone, cable, burglar alarm, internet access, etc.

- **Insurances** - such as life, health (including an amount for co-pays), homeowner/renter's, automobile and long-term-care. The latter is especially important as both you and your parent's age. It is one of the best asset protection devices around.
- **Auto-related Expenses** - including car payment, tags/license, repairs and gasoline
- **Commute** - fares and parking
- **Consumer Loans** - charge accounts, paying off the most expensive debt first
- **Taxes/Fees**
- **Child/Elder Care** - to cover your own expense, plus any support you have committed to give to help provide care for others
- **Food**
- **Clothing**
- **Laundry/Dry Cleaning**
- **Tuition/Student Loan Payments** - for yourself, your children or grandchildren (including any on which you have co-signed)
- **College Funding** – for minor children
- **Entertainment**
- **Vacation(s)**
- **Gifts** – including birthdays, anniversaries, holidays, graduation, etc.
- **Allowance(s)** – for self and for other family members
- **Personal** – such as hair, nails, massages
- **Miscellaneous**

After all known income and expense items are listed and dollar amounts assigned to each, do the calculations to determine whether your desired expenses can be supported by the income expected. If not, then make the needed changes to bring the budget into balance. As I tell clients when they face a shortfall, "For this year, Disney World may have to become Six Flags!"

When one client's 12-month budget showed a serious shortfall of $3,600, I explained to her that either she had to increase her income by that amount or decrease her expenses by a similar amount. She assured me she had no other place she could get the money. There was then only one other option—cut expenses. She didn't like that idea either and assured me there was no place she could cut. When I suggested cutting out the housekeeper, she gasped. "I don't know how to tell her she can't come anymore. She's been coming for so long." My response was, "Don't tell her she can't come; tell her you can't pay her. I guarantee you she'll find someplace else to go every Thursday." (I am Mimi's daughter and chose to give it to her straight.) Eventually, she took my suggestion and let the housekeeper go.

Secure the advice of professional financial experts when you have questions you cannot answer.

Call in the pros, when needed. Don't try to go it alone. Most people who find they are members of the sandwich generation are not finance professionals. Sure, you may have spent years managing the finances of your own nuclear family. However, this is different and may require the help of people a lot more experienced in financial matters than you are. Financial experts - planners, accountants, estate planners, investment advisors and attorneys - may need to be assembled as a team, with each bringing his/her own expertise to the table to help you build a solid, workable plan and to help you prepare for whatever may be over the horizon.

This team may help you do things like figure out where you can cut costs; scrutinize nursing-home bills; set up trusts for yourself or for your parents to minimize estate taxes; prepare a timeline to show when you might expect to have to start financially helping your parents, based on their assets and needs; and restructure investments for your parents so their bills can be paid on time and more easily by using some of their own assets. These professionals are not free nor are their services cheap. However, don't let the cost alone keep you from using them. As the saying goes, "If you think hiring a professional is expensive, wait until you find out, first hand, the cost of hiring an amateur!" (Some cities and counties offer free financial counseling classes and tax preparation services to low-to-moderate-income citizens.)

Meet with a licensed tax preparer to ensure you get all your legal deductions.

Use a tax professional to help you with your own tax return preparation to ensure it fully reflects all the legitimate deductions to which you are entitled. For example, he/she can help determine whether a parent/offspring legally can be taken as a dependent for tax purposes and, if so, calculate that option's benefit. This may include things like the deductibility of your dependent's medical expenses on your own tax return.

According to current law, a family member can be claimed as a dependent on your tax return if two conditions are met. First, the family member's total income must be less than $3,800 for the year, excluding non-taxable Social Security and disability payments. (Interest payments, dividends and withdrawals from retirement accounts all are counted as income.) Second, you must provide more than 50% of the relative's total support. There is no income limit for children.

Once you have determined the relative (parent, spouse, step-parent, sister, grandparent, cousin, aunt or in-law) qualifies as a dependent for tax purposes, there are several dependent expenses that are deductible. These include:

- **Medical costs** - to the extent they meet the annual threshold as defined by the IRS. In 2014, total medical costs must exceed 10% of your adjusted gross income with any excess over that amount being tax deductible. However, if you are 65 or older, the threshold is reduced from 10% to 7.5%. Included here are any unreimbursed medical equipment costs such as wheelchairs, walkers, portable oxygen tanks, diabetes medication and supplies, nebulizers, and the like.

- **Hospitalization costs** - not covered by private insurance or Medicare

- **Out-of-pocket costs for prescription drugs, dental care, co-pays, deductibles, ambulance services and glasses**

- **Long-term-care services**

- **Acupuncture treatments**

- **Weight-loss programs** - if part of the treatment for a specific condition

- **Wigs** - if hair loss is due to a medical condition or medication

- **Adapters** - for televisions, radios and telephones if the relative suffers from hearing loss

- **Smoking- and alcohol-cessation programs**

- **In-home-care costs** - if your relative can't be left alone

- **Housing modifications** - needed for medical reasons, e.g., electric chairs and chair rails, ramps, bathroom safety bars, adaptive furniture, etc.

In addition to the above deductions, another well-kept secret is that you, as the provider of more than 50% of your loved one's care, also may use your own tax-advantaged flexible spending account (FSA) to pay for your dependent family member's covered medical costs. For 2014, the federal cap on FSAs is $2,500, though your own employer's cap might be lower.

As you can tell, there are tax implications and ramifications of many of the decisions you might have to make as you travel the caregiver path. Just be certain you get the information you need to help ensure you make an informed, high-quality decision.

Set up a college fund for your minor dependents as early as possible.

Helping your parents/grandparents is only half the story of you being "squeezed in the financial middle" and is only one side of the equation. Many of you also have minor children and grandchildren who are tugging at your purse strings.

As it relates to helping ensure funds are available for their higher education, once you have made sure you can cover your necessities, you should set up a college fund - a 529 Plan, a pre-paid tuition plan, or some other college savings plan - for your younger dependents as early as possible, even if you contribute only a small amount monthly. (If you set it up as an automatic withdrawal from your paycheck, you won't have to think about it and are more likely to keep up the deposits.) In addition, other family members can contribute to or set up plans for these same minors. An added bonus, depending upon the state in which you live and the plan you choose, is that your contributions may be deductible for state tax purposes, up to the maximum allowed by your state. Go on line to *www.about.com/529+plans+by+state* or get information from *www.Savingforcollege.com* to learn about your state's specific plan.

> **If funds are limited and scholarship help is not readily available, consider having your young dependent start his/her higher education at a community college or in-state school.**

According to data from the U.S. Department of Education's Annual Survey of Colleges covering the period 1987-2008, the increase in published in-state tuition and fees at four-year public colleges was 51% when expressed in 2013 dollars. The increase at four-year, private, non-profit colleges was 25%, and the in-state tuition and fee increase at two-year public colleges was 35%. The average family's income did not keep pace with this soaring cost. In fact, family income has remained almost constant over this period. In some instances, college savings plans like those discussed earlier have been insufficient to cover four years of even the basic college expenses of tuition, fees and room and board.

In addition to the rising costs on one side, many college students are getting out of school with high levels of student loans that have been taken out to finance the funding gap between the cost of education at their school of choice and the financial resources available. For that population, this means high monthly outlays to repay these loans in addition to the regular expenses of daily living, starting families, buying homes and saving for retirement.

Think about various ways to reduce college costs. Involve your young dependents in the school assessment so they have ownership in the final decision. Empower them to make smart education choices.

Consider a community college or state university for at least the first two years. This reduces tuition and possibly eliminates room and board costs if your dependent continues to live at home. You will find these outlays to be dramatically lower than those at a four-year private or out-of-state institution. In many cases, if they choose the right courses, students get full credit for units earned at a community college. There are many community colleges that offer a high-quality education and allow your student to transition smoothly into a four-year institution.

However, though only indirectly related to money, there are several things you want to be sure are handled properly if the minor starts off at a two-year institution versus a four-year college. Here are a few "To Do's" for you:

- Contact the dean of students at the community college being considered to determine what percentage of students completing an associate's degree transfer to a four-year university.

- Call the admissions office of your dependent's target university and ask about the number of transfer students they admit each year and the names of the community colleges with which they have guaranteed admissions agreements. (In the case of a guaranteed admissions agreement, students from a particular community college are guaranteed admission to a four-year partner, if they fully meet the terms and conditions of the agreement.)

- Try to find out which class credits will actually be transferable and will count toward the student's general education. Make sure these are the classes your child enrolls in at the community college. If your student has selected his or her major, determine which classes will count toward that major and make sure they are the classes chosen.

- Have your student register early because classes tend to fill up quickly. You don't want the two-year timeframe to be extended because classes were full.

- Find an adviser at the community college selected who knows and understands the transfer system.

The American Association of Collegiate Registrars and Admissions Officers' website has a state-by-state guide which you might find very useful. The site can be accessed at *www.aaocrao.org.*

> **Have your young loved one consider joining the military to reduce post-secondary-education costs.**

If your child or grandchild is so inclined, military service offers a smorgasbord of education benefits that can be used while he/she is on active duty or after he/she leaves the service. These are generous education benefits he/she will have earned, so it makes sense to take advantage of them.

Active duty service members may get up to $4,500 a year in tuition assistance. The cost of the classes is paid directly to the school on a per-class basis and there is no requirement for an up-front outlay of funds followed by a tuition reimbursement request. Service members also can use benefits of the GI Bill, which is the centerpiece of armed services educational benefits. However, these may be better used after they finish active duty service.

The GI Bill encompasses several Department of Veterans Affairs education programs. Since your loved one may be eligible for more than one educational benefit, knowing the alternative programs available and matching each to his/her situation can save him/her money and ensure he/she gets the most out of the benefits earned. Two other military options to subsidize college costs are ROTC and the reserves and are worth looking into.

To learn more about the large variety of military education benefit options, go to the website *www.military.com/education/gi-bill/guide.*

Grandparents and Education Savings Plans

Instead of applying for student loans, some college students turn to generous sandwich-generation grandparents (you) - many of whom have a higher net worth than their own children. Increasingly, many of you contribute to your grandchildrens' college funds rather than giving outright gifts on birthdays and other special occasions. If you choose to go this route, be aware of the precedent you set with the first grandchild. Your support for one grandchild may set up an expectation of support for others. You don't want saving for your grandkids' college to compromise your own retirement plans.

Consider setting up a prepaid tuition plan, a Section 529 Plan, and/or a Coverdell Education Savings Account. Prepaid tuition plans generally allow you to pay for tuition (and, sometimes, room and board) at today's rates for a student who will attend college in the future. However, many prepaid plans are state-sponsored and are only available to state residents. Alternatively, Section 529 and Coverdell college savings plans are investment accounts that donors contribute to over time whose use is not restricted to local educational institutions. As mentioned, distributions from these two plans aren't subject to federal tax - and sometimes, state tax - as long as they're used to pay for qualifying higher education costs at an eligible institution. Qualifying costs for both plans include college/university tuition, room and board, books and even computers. However, qualifying expenses for Coverdell accounts have been expanded to include primary and secondary schools.

Other Ways to Lower College Costs

Hundreds of millions of dollars of scholarships and grants; tax credits; and benefits go unclaimed every year. Taking advantage of these funds can be complicated, but the payoff can be significant over the course of your student's college career. Both of you - you and your young dependent - should become very familiar with them to minimize your own financial outlay.

- **Scholarships and Fellowships** - If you or your children are fortunate enough to receive a scholarship or fellowship for higher education, that's great news! According to the IRS, scholarship and fellowship money is tax-free if the student is a degree candidate at an eligible educational institution and the money is used for qualified education expenses. Qualified expenses are tuition and fees, books, supplies and equipment required for a class, but they do not include room and board.

  The best place to start your search for college scholarships is to look at those requiring residency in your home state. They provide many of the most generous awards. In addition, you may find valuable information on the following sites:

1. *www.scholarships.com/financial-aid/college-scholarships*

   Provides information on scholarships for incoming freshmen and undergraduates from any state.

2. *www.scholarships.com*

   Provides information on scholarships that are tailored to specific potential applicants based on criteria such as GPA, ACT/SAT scores, athletic ability, etc.

3. *www.bigfuture.collegeboard.org/scholarship-search*

   Offers information on scholarships, financial aid and internships for more than 2,000 programs.

- **Education Tax Credits -** Under certain circumstances, the IRS allows a credit on your tax return through the American Opportunity Tax Credit or Lifetime Learning Tax Credit, depending upon your income level. (Your tax preparer can guide you through the decision-making process to determine if either of these credits applies in your particular situation.) Once the two of you determine if you qualify, then you two can decide which credit would be better to take. Either credit can be taken for yourself, your spouse or your dependent. But, be warned, you can't claim this deduction or credit if your filing status is married filing separately or if another person can claim an exemption for you or your dependent on his/her tax return.

- **Student Loan Interest Deduction** - The IRS allows a deduction for interest on student loans, but there are income caps and other stipulations on this deduction. For you to take a deduction, you must be a signer on the loan documents and be responsible for repayment.

As you can see, there are lots of ways to minimize college expenses. You just need to examine each of them carefully and make full use of the advantages available to you.

Seek help from an elder care attorney if there are significant legal issues to be resolved.

You might be wondering, "What are elder care attorneys? Who do they serve? What do they do? Are they worth the money?" The answer to the last question can be a resounding, "Yes," depending upon the issues that need to be addressed.

The specialty of "elder law" evolved in the 1980s as it became increasingly clear that the complicated legal issues confronting seniors, in particular, qualifying for Medicaid coverage and understanding Medicare rules, were beyond the expertise of general-practice attorneys. In recent years, we've increasingly seen the field described as "elder care law" and the lawyers as "elder care attorneys."

One role an elder care attorney can play is keeping track of laws affecting both Medicare and Medicaid. Other ways they typically help families are:

- Applying for Medicaid coverage of long-term care when the time comes

- Planning and administering an estate

- Representing guardians and conservators

- Creating and administering trusts.

Elder care attorneys are also aware that their clients' needs often extend beyond basic legal services. For this reason, they usually are linked to a network of professionals in their community who serve the senior population.

Anyone can call himself/herself an elder law attorney. Today in the U.S., some 10,000 lawyers claim to practice elder or elder care law. How do you know who is truly qualified? One way is to consult the ElderLawAnswers' directory of member attorneys available through the association's website: *www.naela.org*.

If you are relatively new to the role of having major responsibility for a grandchild, seek out available information on grandparenting.

For many of you sandwich generation-ers, while you may not be new at grandparenting, having major responsibility for a minor child is not something you have done lately. You don't have to do this without backup and support. There are numerous public and private organizations dedicated to helping grandparents fulfill this responsibility.

One such organization that provides a multitude of programs and information is called the **Foundation for Grandparenting** (*www.grandparenting.org*), instituted in 1975. Its stated purpose is " … to provide research, program development, education, communication and networking related to grandparents and their grandchildren." It looks at child, parent, grandparent and great-grandparent issues and also investigates the roles non-biological elders play for children (especially those at-risk). Some of the specific issues examined and closely followed are legal issues, long-distance grand-parenting, and cyber grandparenting.

In addition, many states and universities offer a program called "Grandparenting University" that gives multi-generational families the opportunity to experience college life together during the summer. Go to their website at *www.grandparenting.com* to get more information about the programs offered and to find one at a school near you.

Become familiar with and get help from federal and state social service organizations that offer programs for seniors.

To educate yourself on federal and local programs targeting senior citizens, you might first look at The National Family Caregiver Support Program in your state. Its services are available to adult family members who provide in-home and community care for a person 60 or older, to grandparents and relatives 55 or older who serve as caregivers for children 18 and younger, or for children of any age who have disabilities.

Funds for The National Family Caregiver Support Program come from Title III-E of the Federal Older Americans Act. Resources are allocated to state agencies on aging which then contract with local service providers to deliver a range of services. These services include:

- General information

- Assistance in getting access to services

- Individual counseling

- Organizing support groups and caregiver training

- Respite care

- Supplemental services, including housing improvement; chores; and provision of medical supplies and services

- Legal assistance for caregivers, grandparents or older individuals who are caregivers for relatives

In addition, all states and the federal government offer a wide variety of services targeting senior citizens. Some of the services and websites provide information related to:

- Caregiver resources - *www.aarp.org* (American Association of Retired Persons) ; *www.nfcacares.org* (National Family Caregivers Association)

- Consumer protection for seniors

- Education, jobs and volunteerism

- End-of-life issues

- Money and taxes for seniors, including Medicare and Medicaid

- Legal - *www.naela.com* (National Association of Elder Care Attorneys); *www.abanet.org/public-html* (American Bankers Association)

- Retirement

- Travel and Recreation

- Grandparents raising children:

    ❖ AARP Grandparents Information Center

    ❖ Social Security benefits for grandchildren

    ❖ The Grandparents Foundation - *www.grandparentsfoundation.com/*

    ❖ The Children's Bureau - *www.acf.hhs.gov/*

- Federal and State agencies for seniors and veterans:

    ❖ Administration on Aging - *www.aoa.gov*

    ❖ NIH Senior Health - *www.nihseniorhealth.gov*

    ❖ Social Security Administration - *ww.ssa.gov/onlineservices/*

    ❖ Veterans Health Administration - *www.va.gov*

As you can see, there are loads of federal, local and private sector organizations out there to support you at every step along your way. You do not have to take this trip alone. (See Appendix D for more resource information.)

The decision to leave the workforce early to care for a loved one can be a difficult one to make. If you choose to do so, try to understand the total financial cost to you.

If you decide to stop working to provide the support needed to care for a loved one, the financial cost to you is certain to be more than just your salary, although that could be a significant amount. For example, if you retire at age 56 instead of your full retirement age of 66, you'll lose 10 years of wages. If you make, say $80,000 a year, that adds up to $800,000. But even that's not the full salary you'd likely give up. During those 10 years, you'd probably get several cost-of-living or merit increases. If you average a 3% annual salary increase, you'd be making over $100,000 a year by the time you reach full retirement age. So, you're really facing close to $1 million in lost salary. Granted, you'd have to pay taxes along the way but, it's still a significant amount of money and a lot more than you'd have if you stop working.

Even if you don't actually retire early, but take an extended leave to care for a loved one, the cost still can be quite high. According to the director of the MetLife Mature Market Institute, " … the average worker who takes time off to provide care for an aging parent sacrifices more than $300,000 in lost wages."

Not only will leaving the workforce early cause you to lose the accumulation of wages, but also there are employee perks that will go away as well as other significant "costs" to that decision. These might include:

- **Employee benefits** - If you're not working, the company will no longer contribute to your 401(k). In addition, you will lose any company-subsidized perks such as discounts; use of fitness equipment, computers, and cell phones; staff lunches; and the like. The average employee gets almost 40% of their salary in the form of extra benefits. For the $80,000 employee, that's an additional $32,000 a year, every year, for the next 10 years. (That amount includes your medical benefits discussed next.)

- **Your employer-subsidized health care benefit** - If you get health insurance through your employer, you benefit from a group rate and a tax-free premium subsidy from your employer. If you retire before the Medicare eligibility age of 65, unless you have medical insurance through an early retirement contract, you will have to buy your own policy. The Affordable Care Act may make health insurance less expensive for some people, but paying for your insurance yourself could easily cost you between $500 and $1,000 a month. (The cost of the insurance may be deductible on your tax return if you itemize deductions, typically on Schedule A, and exceed the current-year's deductible threshold.)

- **Lower Social Security benefits** - Social Security reduces your monthly check by approximately 7% for every year early you start to draw social security benefits. If you elect to begin to receive your payments at 62, the youngest age of eligibility, you give up about 25% of the monthly benefit you would have gotten if you had waited a few more years to retire with full retirement benefits. **Those who wait beyond age 66/67 will enjoy an 8% annual increase in benefits until age 70. After that, there is no further advantage to delaying benefits.**

  Since it is true that you could receive benefits for a longer period of time if you start at age 62, in the end, the amount might equal out *if* you live long enough. That doesn't help when you're trying to pay your bills with $1,000 a month instead of the higher $1,250 a month you would have received had you waited until age 66/67. Also, you're stuck with those lower payments for the rest of your life!

You may be giving up resources you'll wish you had later. Instead of using your prime earning years to build up your savings, with early retirement you'll be spending down those savings sooner rather than later. As a result, you'll have a smaller nest egg when you get to your "golden years." Maybe you don't think money will matter much then because by the time you're in your 70s, 80s and

90s, you think you will be too old to need much of it. Only time will tell.

The Department of Health and Human Services' Administration on Aging's statistics show not only are we living longer, but also, we are living healthier, more active lifestyles. The average life expectancy is now 77 for men and 82 for women. Today, there is a 41% chance that a 62-year-old woman will live to age 90. A 62-year-old man has a 29% chance of living to that same age. For a married couple, there is a 58% chance that one of them will live to 90 and a 29% chance one will reach the ripe old age of 95!

Even with living healthier, in those later years, you will likely have medical bills and living costs, and will still want to be able to provide for a roof over your head. I'm not trying to frighten you. I just want you to fully consider the ramifications of a decision to retire early.

It may be possible to do so if you plan ahead, watch your spending and settle for a more modest lifestyle. Just be aware that the price tag for early retirement is high. It may be worth it for some, but not for everybody.

To minimize the cost of your decision to retire early, delay, for as long as possible, drawing your retirement benefits.

According to a recent survey sponsored by the Lincoln Retirement Institute, " … If offered a chance to travel back in time, many baby boomers would change their planning strategy for retirement. Most expressed a wish for a "do over" with more than a quarter saying they would tell their younger selves to start saving for retirement sooner."

In addition to making the mistakes of not starting to save early enough and having no retirement plan at all, financial planners seem to agree that another huge financial mistake both boomers and sandwich generation-ers make is retiring too early! For many who feel "squeezed" and are looking for a way to get the time needed to deal with the pressures of multi-generational living and responsibilities, an obvious answer is to get out of the workforce. They think being no longer tied to the nine-to-five grind would mean more time to deal with the multitude of issues they have to confront each day.

In 2008, the oldest of the 79 million baby boomers turned 62. This group is projected to live longer than any previous generation of Americans. They also will have the longest retirements.

A major question for you to answer is whether you can meet your financial needs with the lower level of resources. Over time, not only will taking benefits early mean a smaller payout, but also it could mean a higher risk of outliving your money. A senior pension fellow with The American Society of Actuaries has calculated that retirees who file for Social Security at age 62 and live until their mid-90s could lose as much as $150,000 in benefits. So, spending down other assets first in order to delay starting to receive Social Security may be a better option.

In addition to the lower Social Security payments, some analysts also advise retirees to delay withdrawing money from their 401(k), IRA and other retirement savings accounts as long as possible. That way, their investments can continue to grow and compound, tax free. The tax bite on those withdrawals could be huge! The taxes were originally designed to target wealthy seniors. But, for some reason, the income thresholds were not indexed for inflation. As a result, the tax now affects middle-income retirees.

There is no cookie-cutter solution to this problem. Each individual should sit down with his/her tax preparer and financial planner to work out the best next steps.

> **To generate additional cash flow, consider refinancing your mortgage to lower your payment.**

For years, mortgage rates have been at or near historic lows. If you're wondering whether to refinance your home loan, you're not alone. It's hard to know exactly when to refinance. The three main objectives of refinancing are to: 1) save money; 2) raise cash; and 3) cut back on your monthly outlays. Following are some things to consider before you actually refinance.

1. **Interest rates**

   A general guideline for deciding whether to refinance is if you can get your interest rate lowered by at least 1½ to 2 percentage points. These figures are generally accepted as the safe margin when determining whether the savings from refinancing a mortgage are worth the cost.

2. **Length of time you plan to stay in your home**

   To find out how long it will take to recover refinancing fees, divide the total cost of refinancing by the amount you'll save on your mortgage payment each month. The resulting number is the length of time, in months, that it will take to break even. If you plan to stay in your current home longer than this amount of time, refinancing may be a good idea.

3. **Your loan type**

   Saving money is only one of the benefits of refinancing your mortgage loan. Another reason many people refinance is to change the type of loan they have. Some customers start out with an adjustable-rate mortgage (ARM) loan to take advantage of the low initial rate, then refinance into a fixed-rate product before the rate increases at the end of the adjustment period. If you have an ARM, especially one with a balloon payment due at the end of the loan period, refinancing may be a viable option.

4. The amount of home equity you have

Another reason many homeowners choose to refinance is to build equity faster or to leverage the equity they already have. When you refinance a 30-year loan into a 15-year loan, you'll build equity twice as fast. This refinance strategy also helps you save money in interest because it will only take you half the time to pay off your loan.

On the other hand, if you've already built some equity in your home, you can tap into it to help fund education, home improvements or unexpected expenses. With this strategy, you may refinance your mortgage loan for more than you currently owe to get access to the cash you need. Be sure the equity pulled out will be to pay for something tangible like a home purchase, a major home repair/remodeling effort or educational expenses rather than an intangible like credit card debt.

While doing a radio call-in show on the subject of finances, I took a call from a listener who said she had lots of equity in her home and had $50,000 worth of credit card debt. She wanted to know whether I thought she should take $50,000 in equity out of her home to pay off that debt. My response was an unequivocal NO! Experience shows that if the money is used to pay off creditors, you are likely to be back in that same position within a couple of years. The debt was not accumulated all at once; so, if it is repaid in one lump sum, you will not have experienced the pain and discipline of sacrificing, changing your habits, and *paying it off slowly, so it is likely to reappear within a few short years.*

Before you make the final decision to refinance, you need to know whether it's truly worth it. First, go to *www.cnnmoney.com* and run the numbers. Then decide.

5. Your credit score

Your credit score at the time you applied for your current mortgage was a critical element in the decision whether to make you the loan requested, the amount of the loan, and the interest rate. If your score has improved significantly since taking out the loan (and overall rates have come down), it may be a good time to refinance your home.

Requesting annual credit reports from the major credit bureaus can help you monitor your credit and decide if and when to refinance. While, legally, the credit reports are free annually from each of the three major credit bureaus, there is usually a fee associated with getting the actual credit score. (See Appendix D for contact information for each of the three major credit bureaus - Equifax, TransUnion and Experian.) Be warned, some highly advertised websites imply they offer "free credit reports" when, in actuality, there is a fee associated with most of their products.

6. PMI

If your loan balance is more than 80% of your home's value, mortgage industry practice is that the lender requires something called PMI, which stands for private mortgage insurance. (It is insurance your lender buys to ensure that a person with less than 20% "skin in the game" will not walk away from the loan. If the borrower does walk, then the insurer will pay your lender any losses incurred up to the policy limit.) When the balance falls below 80%, PMI is no longer required and usually can be dropped if you make a specific request from the lender. (It does not happen automatically. You must initiate and complete the sometimes tedious paperwork process with your lender.) Eliminating PMI doesn't always require refinancing, but refinancing your home when your equity has grown substantially can remove this unnecessary (and costly) expense. At the same time, you may be able to restructure your loan for a lower rate or for a different term.

7. Your loan term

If your goal is to build equity in your home quickly and your budget can support a higher monthly payment, you may consider refinancing to a shorter-term mortgage. A shorter loan term means that you'll own your home debt-free sooner and pay less in interest over the course of the loan. As an added bonus, you can access that extra equity later for an emergency or a large purchase through some type of home equity loan. You can also build equity in your home faster by making extra principal payments or by making 13 payments per year rather than the standard 12. It is said that a 30-year mortgage can be paid off in about 22 years by consistently making that 13th payment each year.

The paperwork required to refinance can be intimidating and tedious. But, under some circumstances, it may be entirely worth it.

Now that we've gotten you to do the things necessary to take care of you, let's see what you need to do to help the other two legs of this three-legged stool stay upright. Next, we'll look at what you may have to do to take care of the older generation - those who once took care of you.

III. TAKING CARE

of the

OLDER GENERATION

(Helping them travel their path with

dignity and grace)

What Would Mimi Say

about

Taking Care of the Older Generation?

❖ One good turn deserves another.

❖ It's a poor rule that only works one way.

❖ Where there's a will, there's a way.

❖ You've got to have hope for a better tomorrow.

❖ God grant me the serenity to accept the things I cannot change; the courage to change the things I can; and the wisdom to know the difference.

Taking Care

of the

Older Generation

Now that we've talked about you and how to take care of yourself, let's focus on one of the other two components of the sandwich - the older generation. The intent here is to give you the tools needed to have you both lighten your own load and treat these loved ones in such a way that they travel this (sometimes uncomfortable) path gracefully, maintaining their dignity along the way. You can do it and, with your help, so can they. As Mimi said, "Where there's a will, there's a way."

Many of you reading this are either baby boomers (born between 1946 and 1964) or Generation X members (born between 1965 and 1980) and have been raised by parents who presented themselves as being strong, healthy and fully in charge. As a result, if and when the day comes when this no longer appears to be the case, it may be hard to recognize, hard to accept and hard to deal with, on both sides. The reality is you may have to learn the signs so you can recognize the need, accept what is before you, and then deal with it if and when you have to.

As baby boomers age, Generation Xer's are comprising more and more of the sandwich generation, and are likely to have a parent over 65 and to be supporting an adult or minor child. The "older" baby boomers are now becoming senior citizens and are the parents who need looking out for. The U.S. Census Bureau predicts our over 65 population will more than double to 92 million by 2060. Furthermore, it expects that 6% of Americans ages 25 to 35 will live in multi-generational housing by then. Mimi would have you say the Serenity Prayer; accept the things you cannot change; change the things you can; and have the wisdom to know the difference. Then, deal with it as best you can. No one can ask any more of you than that.

Almost 75% of respondents to a 2012 Pew Research Survey said that providing financial and other assistance to aging parents in need is a responsibility they have to their parents. By comparison, only 52% said parents have this same level of responsibility when it comes to supporting a grown child. However, slightly less than 25% have been called upon to do so recently.

In the Pew Survey, this strong sentiment, especially for providing financial support, was felt across demographic, ideological, racial and political lines. However, when it came to age groups, that's where the lines separated. Adults under 40 felt a slightly greater responsibility to support aging parents than those considered "middle aged" - 40 to 59 - (81% versus 75%). This compares to only 68% of adults over 60, some of whom themselves are beginning to feel the ravages of age, who feel the same level of responsibility.

Other Pew Survey results about providing (or expecting to provide) financial assistance to aging parents showed distinct differences among various groups. For example:

- Demographically, Hispanic and Blacks were more likely than Whites to have already provided financial assistance to a parent over age 65. Also, there were vast differences in expectations. 64% of Hispanics said they expect to provide some type of care for an aging family member in the future compared to 48% of Blacks and 43% of Whites.

- Those with household incomes under $75,000 were more likely to be supporting aging parents over 65 than those with higher household incomes.

- More aid is given to aging Mothers than to aging Fathers.

- While only 3% of adults younger than 40 have provided this type of assistance, 62% expect to do so at some point in the future.

- Married respondents were more likely to expect to do so than singles (75% versus 60%). In part, this could be due to now having two sets of parents to deal with.

- Nearly half (46%) of baby boomers with at least one parent over age 80 indicated having a parent needing care.

The Pew Survey results are interesting and provide a backdrop for the subject at hand - whether, when and how to provide financial management assistance to the "older generation." For most of you, this is an area where you must tread very gently. The strain on you and the financial burdens that come with caring for multiple generations can be both staggering and overwhelming and, if not handled properly, can have a negative impact on your own household's well-being. For purposes of this exercise, we will focus primarily on the financial matters you need to pay careful attention to as they relate to this "older generation" and offer some money secrets to try to help smooth your path and lighten your load, and theirs.

How do you know when an aging parent or other family member needs help managing their finances?

According to Family Care America, there are several signs you can look for to try to determine whether your aging family member might need help with managing his/her money. Such signs include noticing whether your loved one:

- Follows a monthly budget

- Keeps up with and understands banking transactions

- Pays all of his/her outstanding liabilities on time

- Appears to use credit responsibly

- Keeps track of important financial and medical records

- Is facing legal actions such as a bankruptcy, eviction or any other court-ordered process

- Consistently bounces checks

- Has had utilities cut off

- No longer understands benefits statements sent by medical insurance companies

- Makes seemingly inappropriate/large/frequent payments to individuals or companies for "undelivered" products or services

- Becomes more secretive about financial matters

Once you've made these observations and gathered this information, you will likely have an idea whether help is needed and/or concern is warranted. But, you haven't finished yet with your "sleuthing." Keep reading.

If answers to any of the above cause you concern, how do you know whether this represents a change in the way he/she used to handle their finances?

To know whether things have changed, first, you need to have a baseline understanding of what is "normal" for them. This requires many conversations to uncover details of their financial (and non-financial) life, much of which they may not be eager to share, especially given their belief that they are still fully able to manage on their own.

Early on, you need to engage them in conversations to try to gather information such as the following:

- Names and locations of financial institutions used

- Location of cancelled checks and bank statements

- ATM cards and PINs

- Credit cards names and numbers

- Certificates of Deposit (locations, amounts, maturity dates)

- Name and phone number of investment advisors, accountants, tax preparers, and lawyers, if there are any

- Location of past tax returns (for at least three years)

- Name of mortgage holder (s), if any

So, begin to educate yourself about your loved one's finances. But, first, make sure they understand that you have their best interest at heart.

> **Although not necessarily financial in nature, what other pieces of related information will you want to talk to your loved one about so you will have a clear idea of how to proceed if the need arises?**

You will find the following information to be particularly valuable if your loved one becomes incapacitated:

- Passwords to all online accounts (financial and non-financial)

- A list of medical professionals used, along with contact information, and the names of all medications currently being taken along with prescription expiration dates (updated regularly and easily accessible)

- Current and historical medical records for hospital, E/R and doctor's visits

- Medical and life insurance providers, premiums charged and current status, including payment dates

- Whether there is a current long-term-care insurance policy and, if so, with whom (This topic is discussed in detail in Chapter VI.)

- Status/location/copy of estate planning and other legal documents such as Wills, Trusts, Powers of Attorney and Advance Medical Directives

- Name of personal representative or executor chosen to handle estate matters

- Eligibility for Medicare and/or Medicaid

- Eligibility for other social services

- Automobile titles

- Deeds to properties owned

- A list of the contents of the safe deposit box, its location and a key

In Chapter VI, elder care attorney, Jacqueline Byrd, joins me to discuss several factors related to the long-term care of your elders. In the first section she looks at how to have "the talk" with your elders to discuss their long-term-care preferences and needs. In the second piece, she writes about factors to consider when choosing a nursing home. Finally, Ms. Byrd and I collaborate to update you on long-term-care insurance and its features, along with a description of care payment options and the roles of Medicare and Medicaid.

> **If, based on all the conversations you have held and the information gathered, you determine your loved one indeed needs help, then what?**

This is where things can get tricky. Understand, this person has lived a life of independence and probably will not be anxious either to give it up or even to share it with someone else. They may still believe they are perfectly capable of caring for themselves. Not only must you determine whether help is needed, but also how to broach the subject with them, and how much and what kind of help is warranted at this point.

Remember, being able to handle their own financial affairs is very much a sign of their independence, and your request to take over all or a part of these duties may not be well received. In any case, it needs to be handled carefully. This means different things for different people. If your loved one tends to be direct, then you may be able to ask your questions and talk about your concerns head on. On the other hand, if you think they would not be able to handle the direct approach well, you may have to go about getting the information differently including asking more general questions, talking about your own experiences or even making up stories about bad experiences others have had when they have not been able to pay full attention to their own finances. Whatever approach you choose, always be respectful and make it clear that you want to help.

Options about the type and amount of help that may be needed include:

- Occasional review of your loved one's financial affairs

- Assistance with bill paying, check writing and checkbook balancing

- Scheduling professional appointments and ensuring they get to them

- For safety reasons, installing of a First Alert-type system, in case emergency help is needed

- Combining households

- Consideration of a nursing home or long-term-care facility (permanently or temporarily)

All but the last two above may be relatively easy. The action to combine two households may be economical and convenient, but it can mean a whole new way of living and a totally new family dynamic for both your loved one and your nuclear family. This is true regardless of whether the loved one will need physical and emotional support, in-home care, or just frequent checking in on to ensure he/she is alright. Your family will likely find it intrusive, and your loved one may feel isolated (from his/her old space, as well as from long-time friends and neighbors) and a loss of privacy.

The choice to put a loved one in either a nursing home or a long-term-care facility is a major decision. You may feel angry, distraught and guilty admitting the inevitability of this choice. Your loved one may feel cast aside, unloved and a whole host of other emotions, all of which point toward major resistance. So, once again, implementation of this decision must be handled very carefully.

If you determine the time has come to move your loved one to a nursing or assisted-living facility of some kind, both the facility's cost and the selection process are major matters that must be dealt with. In addition, you must have a full understanding of your loved one's finances to know whether he/she is eligible for government assistance, has his/her own personal resources, or expect you to pay all or part of the cost out of your own funds.

According to Genworth Life Insurance Company, a provider of long-term-care insurance for over 50 years, the aging baby boomer population in the U.S. is approaching 80 million. They project that more than 70% of seniors over 65 will need long-term-care support and services at some point in their lives. This can have a major financial impact on the seniors themselves as well as those who love and care for them. The result of Genworth's 2014 Cost of Care Survey covering almost 15,000 long-term-care providers in over 400 regions nationwide found that the national cost for a private room in a nursing facility is $83,790 per year. Home care is much less expensive and most seniors would prefer being cared for at home, if possible. If unplanned for, care expenses may put a huge dent in the caregiver's personal savings and may impact their current and future retirement resources as well.

My friend Cara's Mother had her own resources but began to make questionable financial choices. It turned out that she was in the early stages of dementia. One clear sign was the large quantity of unneeded, similar items she was purchasing, almost daily, from television ads and infomercials. (Customer service representatives from many of the advertisers knew her by name.) Yet, she refused to turn over either her credit cards or her checkbook to her only child to manage believing she could still handle her own affairs. Much later, when it became clear she was unable to manage on her own, Cara prevailed, but not before she spent an entire summer cataloging the unopened packages stored in her Mother's house and finding charities to which to donate them.

After much consideration, Cara and her husband decided to sell both their house and her Mother's house and purchased one big enough for the multi-generational family to live in comfortably. (Cara also had an adult son with a medical disability living at home.) The house was large enough to provide space for a live-in home health care aide when her Mother's illness became more severe. Though a difficult and costly situation to deal with, when the end came, Cara found peace in knowing that she had done everything she could have for her Mom. Her friends and colleagues knew it too.

In Appendix D, there is a list of web resources related to care giving as well as resources regarding print material on the same subject. The National Caregiver's Library is one of the most complete guides to information resources on the topic of care giving. Visit *www.caregiverslibrary.com* for more information.

Does your loved one have and stick to a budget?

If your loved one has the ability to operate financially independently, do they have their finances organized in the form of a budget? If so, is it complete, i.e., does it fully account for all expected income and expenses? If not, this could be a sign that his/her finances are not as orderly as they should be.

Because we want to be certain financial resources are being conserved and need to understand whether there are sufficient funds to support his/her desired lifestyle, it is critically important that this person has a roadmap that provides a complete picture of their expected income and expenses for at least the next 12 months and contains items that reflect whatever reality they will be living. This is the only way you can understand whether there is a funding shortfall and whether you are the person who would be expected to bridge any gap.

If they will continue to live independently, though it may contain items that are different than those in your own, following are the types of items that should be included in theirs.

Income sources might include:

- Social Security income
- Retirement income
- Net income from regular or part-time job
- Investment and dividend income
- Tax refunds (federal and state)
- Gifts

In other words, as was the case with yours, their budget should include every dollar of income they expect to receive.

In the "Expense" section of their budget, following is a list of the types of expenses you will want to include:

- **Donations/Tithing** - at whatever level they can comfortably afford
- **Mortgage/Rent Payments** - depending upon whether they are a homeowner or a renter
- **Taxes**
- **Home Repairs** (for homeowners)
- **Utilities** - including water, gas/electric, home phone, cell phone, cable, burglar alarm, etc.
- **Insurances** - such as life, health (including an amount for co-pays), homeowner/renter's, automobile and long-term-care.

67

- **Auto-related Expenses** - including car payment, tags/license, repairs, gasoline
- **Charge Accounts/Loans**
- **Food**
- **Clothing**
- **Laundry**
- **Entertainment**
- **Vacation(s)**
- **Gifts** - including birthdays, anniversaries, holidays, graduation, etc.
- **Allowance**
- **Miscellaneous**

Once developed, you might consider regularly reviewing the budget with them to determine 1) whether it really represents their income and expense patterns, and 2) the extent to which they are following the plan. If either of the above is not true, then you will want to work with them to develop needed adjustments and to determine whether a financial commitment from you or others is warranted. Obviously, if it is, then, you may have to take the lead in working with family members to determine the contribution each can and is willing to make. For you, it may mean a financial adjustment to your own budget, standard of living and retirement plans.

If your loved one still lives independently, what are ways to save him/her money and to cut expenses?

Regardless of the lifestyle your loved one wants to lead, there are always opportunities to conserve expenditures, thereby increasing the dollars available to save or to spend for his/her own other needs and wants. It is critically important to choose a realistic, affordable lifestyle - one that does not cause your loved one to outlive his/her resources.

Following are just a few of the many "money secrets" (compiled by AARP in its annual survey) that you might want to share with your family members (or even use for yourself):

- Install a programmable thermostat. Such an instrument can save hundreds of dollars a year in energy costs.

- Buy movie tickets in multiples, especially from a big box store or from the theater's corporate website. Many seniors enjoy going to the movies as a simple, relaxing, safe form of entertainment.

- Install low-flow showerheads. According to the EPA, doing so can save thousands of gallons of water per year, resulting in lower water costs.

- If still working, have them take lunch to work at least a couple of days each week, thereby minimizing the cost of eating lunch out.

- Attend free lectures at local colleges and universities to keep the brain stimulated.

- If they have both a land line and a cell phone, look at whether one of the two, most often the land line, can be eliminated unless there is a home security system tied to the land line. If the decision is made to keep both lines activated, closely examine the bills of each to see whether any of the services being paid for are going unused and, thus, can be eliminated. Also, see whether any of the organizations they belong to have relationships with cell phone providers that offer member discounts.

- To try to cut down on medical expenses, eat more healthily and exercise more. Often, free exercise classes for seniors are offered at local community/recreation centers.

- If available and their doctor approves, use lower-cost generic versus brand name drugs. This can lead to great savings on medical expenses. Also, if available, economize on prescriptions by making bulk mail-order purchases.

- To get rid of the temptation, eliminate "window shopping."

- Look for restaurants and other retail establishments that offer "free" drinks and discounts to seniors, especially those to who show AARP cards. These discounts are available at Denny's, Michaels, IHOP and Amtrack, to name a few.

- Make sure to sign up for Medicare within the penalty-free time period. (This means different things to different people. But, contact Medicare to determine what it means for your loved one.) To enroll late will result in a **permanent** penalty of up to 10% for each month of late registration.

- If affordable and if it makes sense given your family's history and your loved one's health, consider having your loved one delay the start of receiving Social Security until the age of 70 to receive the maximum benefit.

- Consider signing up for a streaming service like Netflix, which is relatively inexpensive and offers unlimited movies and TV shows. It can be a wonderful source of entertainment.

- Cancel most, if not all, magazine subscriptions.

- Cut back on at least one personal service each month. Things like hairdos, massages, manicures, pedicures, lip/eyebrow wax and facials all qualify and will generate extra funds if cut back on.

- Check out the discount coupon websites such as *www.retailmenot.com*; *www.groupon.com*; and *www.opentable.com*. These sites offer a variety of common products and discounts and have the potential of saving you and your loved one lots of money.

How do I protect an aging loved one from scam artists?

It is critical that you inform him/her about possible scams and what to be on the lookout for as part of the care you provide. According to AARP, statistically, the elderly lose more money to scams than any other demographic (though they are not the only victims).

Why are seniors such a ready target? The reasons include:

- Fear

- Frailty of aging

- Dependence on others

- Isolation

These factors cause the perpetrators to feel they can engage in scams and that they will go either undetected or unreported. In many cases, this is true. In reality, however, it only gives them the confidence to become more and more aggressive.

Unfortunately, the perpetrators of these scams include some people victims would least likely suspect:

- Family members/friends - who the senior knows and trusts and to whom the senior wants to stay connected

- Caregivers - who take advantage of those seniors who they have been entrusted to care for

- Strangers - who may be preying on those who feel isolated, confused or lonely

So, you see why it is so important that you spend lots of time educating your loved one about the possibility of scams and the types of things to be on the lookout for. At the same time, you should monitor his/her activities and accounts to be on the watch for any signs of that person being taken advantage of. If you have even an inkling that something is awry, then you should take immediate steps to alert the proper authorities to have both the scam and the scam artist stopped.

What are some of the top scams targeting seniors that you can make sure your loved one is aware of?

While there have been numerous scams perpetrated against seniors, following is a list of those deemed by the National Council on Aging to be most prevalent:

- **Telemarketing** - This is the most common scam of all. It occurs when scammers make fake telemarketing calls to seniors who, as a group, make twice as many purchases over the phone as the national average. With only telephone contact and no paper trail, these scams are hard to trace. Often, after a deal is made, scammers then share the buyer's name with other scammers, sometimes resulting in repeated defrauding of the same victim.

- **Sweepstakes/Lottery Scams** - Scammers advise the target that they have won a prize that requires money to be sent to "claim the prize." Often a phony check is sent to the senior who then deposits the check in his/her account. By the time the check bounces, the scammer has pocketed the money the victim has sent and has moved on to the next mark.

- **The Grandparent Scam** - In this scam, scammers place a call to an older person and pretend to be a grandchild or other family member in need of money to resolve some immediate and unexpected financial need. The unsuspecting senior is then asked to wire the funds via Western Union or Money Gram (neither of which always requires identification to collect). The scammer asks the senior to please not tell his/her parents so there is no one else in the family or close to the senior who is made aware of this fraudulent transaction. Thus, it goes unmentioned and unreported, and is perpetrated over and over by the scammer at very little cost or risk.

- **Internet Fraud** - Seniors' relative unfamiliarity with internet intricacies makes them ripe targets for internet scams. Pop-up browser windows simulating virus scanning/virus protection software, fake anti-virus programs or an actual virus that takes over a senior's computer and makes whatever information is on it available to scammers are all ways such crooks gain illegal access to personal data to which they have no right.

- **Reverse Mortgage Scam** - Scammers offer the senior money or a free house someplace else in exchange for the title to their property. Once the title is turned over to the scammer, the target either does not receive the money promised or is placed in a house not owned by the scammer.

- **Counterfeit Prescription Drugs** - Most of these scams operate on the internet where seniors often go to get better prices on their medication. In addition to the possibility of getting "medication" at a lower price, there is the danger that the senior may purchase unsafe medications that bring even greater harm to their bodies.

- **Funeral and Cemetery Scams** - In one tactic, scammers read obituaries and call or attend the funeral services of a complete stranger to take advantage of the grieving spouse. Claiming the deceased had an outstanding debt with them, the scammer then tries to extort money from relatives to settle fake debts. In another, disreputable funeral homes try to capitalize on family members' unfamiliarity with the cost of funeral services to add charges to the bill.

- **Fraudulent Anti-aging Products** - In their quest to maintain a youthful appearance, many seniors are willing to go to great expense to get the look of the "young and beautiful." Thus, there is lots of money in the anti-aging business. Not only are seniors often conned out of their money by buying products that do not work, but also, the health consequences of products such as fake Botox can be very harmful.

- **Health Care/Medicare Insurance Fraud** - According to the Centers for Medicare and Medicaid Services, total health care expenditures in the U.S. are expected to reach over $2.25 trillion by 2016. It is expected that as the expenditures grow, so will the fraud and correspondingly the work of the FBI - the government agency charged with investigating insurance fraud and abuse.

Health insurance fraud comes in many different forms - fraudulent billings, unnecessary medical services, duplicate claims, unneeded prescriptions, kickbacks, etc. They target both public and private health care programs, and individuals. Given that Medicare and Medicaid are the largest public programs, it comes as no surprise that they are targeted more often than most programs. The same can be said of their subscribers. Medicare scams are some of the biggest frauds confronting seniors. In most of them, Medicare is billed for products and services never delivered. Following are safeguards seniors can execute:

❖ Protect your Medicare number/card (usually your social security number) just as you would a credit card and never allow anyone else to use it.

❖ Review Medicare statements for accuracy to ensure the billing covers services actually received.

❖ Be wary of salespeople trying to sell you a product or service they claim will be paid for by Medicare.

❖ Never sign a blank insurance claim form.

❖ Beware of free health services. (Mimi says, "You don't get something for nothing.")

❖ Review all of your medical bills and explanation-of-benefits statements to be certain you have actually received the services billed at the cost agreed upon in advance.

❖ Ensure all service dates are correct.

❖ Report anything you find suspicious to **1-800-MEDICARE**

- **Charity Scams** - Money is solicited for fake charities. This often occurs after natural disasters or high-profile crimes where funds are supposedly being collected to aid the victims. Often the collector has no connection whatever to the victims.

  A participant in a financial literacy class I taught in 2001 was the Mother of one of the students on the plane that hit the Pentagon on 9/11. We had been discussing scam artists when she raised her hand. I recognized her and the story she told was chilling.

  According to her, shortly after 9/11, she went out to a local shopping mall to find a dress to wear to her son's funeral. As she was walking to her car, a female beggar approached her and said her son had been on the plane that hit the Pentagon and she was trying to collect enough money to bury him. The Mother asked this woman her son's name. The name the woman gave her was none other than that of HER own son! She said to the scammer, "Oh, no he wasn't! That was MY son! The woman then ran off and was not seen again. (The names of the victims of 9/11 was public information.)

  So, you can see, we all have to be careful, vigilant and smart. None of us wants to be taken advantage of.

- **Investment Schemes** - Many seniors are looking for a safe place to stash their retirement savings for access in their later years. Scammers know this and use various scams and schemes to get their hands on the ready pot of cash many seniors are holding. Bernie Madoff's Ponzi Scheme was a shining example of such a scam. You should perform the necessary due diligence to make certain the financial personnel with whom you and your loved ones are working are legitimate.

What are some tips to avoiding Telemarketing scams?

What advice can you give your loved one to minimize the probability of him/her becoming a victim of a telemarketing scam?

- Don't buy from a company that you have never heard of and know nothing about without checking it out both on the internet and with the Better Business Bureau.

- Before you act, always insist on information in writing rather than just over the phone and do not commit until you have received and reviewed it.

- Ask lots of questions and take whatever time is needed to get other opinions and to do any needed research **before** making a commitment.

- Get, in writing, a salesperson's identifying information prior to making a "buy" decision.

Several other Common Scams are discussed in Chapter VII.

What are some tips to help prevent your loved one from falling prey to marketing scams?

As part of their advice to elderly citizens to help them avoid being victimized by junk mail and marketing scams, the National

Council on Aging advises that we give our senior loved ones the following advice (or do it for them):

- Avoid filling in marketing surveys or questionnaires. Junk mailers buy this information to send junk mail, unsolicited e-mails, and to make telephone calls that are likely to result in high sales.

- Have their name removed from directories such as *www.192.com* because businesses use directories like this one to obtain names and addresses legitimately. However, consumers can request to have their information removed, thereby making their name and contact information less readily available.

- Write "Unsolicited Mail; Return to Sender" on junk mail with a return address on it and put it back in the postal system without postage. This may increase the mailer's costs and discourage them from continuing to send mail to that address.

- When filling out the annual election form, suggest they check the box that indicates that they do not want to be added to the "Edited Electoral Register."

- Never respond to a suspicious e-mail or bogus telephone call.

- Check the "opt out" box to indicate they don't want any further information about "other products and services" when they have to provide their names/addresses to businesses.

- Do not provide callers/e-mailers with any information, be it personal or financial.

Even with taking these careful steps, there still is no guarantee that fraudulent attempts will not be made. One just has to remain alert and to try to stay at least one step ahead of the bad guys.

If your loved one is a veteran, are there medical services for which he/she and family members are eligible? If so, are they available at discounted rates?

If your loved one is a veteran, he/she and family members might be eligible for discounted or free medical and/or nursing home services. If the need arises for hospital care, though they are sometimes seen as quite bureaucratic, the quality of medical care at Veterans Affairs hospitals is generally viewed as quite good and these hospitals are very inexpensive. Depending upon the level of support for which the veteran qualifies, no additional medical coverage may be needed.

Those retired from uniformed service are eligible to receive expanded medical coverage through a program called TRICARE, formerly known as the Civilian Health and Medical Program of the Uniformed Services (CHAMPUS). It provides civilian health benefits for military personnel, military retirees, and their dependents, including some members of the reserve component. TRICARE is the civilian care component of the Military Health System. To get detailed information on this program, go on line to *www.tricareonline.com.*

The most complete source of information on services offered, eligibility requirements, pricing, procedures and forms needed is available by calling the Department of Veterans Affairs or going onto their website at *www.va.gov.* To determine whether your loved one is eligible for free or low-cost nursing home care, you may also call your local veterans affairs office. Other veteran resource sites are listed in Appendix D - Resources.

The seniors you are trying to help clearly are people who mean a lot to you. If they didn't, you wouldn't be going through the effort to help organize various aspects of their lives to make whatever time they have left as comfortable and as hassle-free as possible. Many have loved and cared about you for a long time. You are to be commended for recognizing when it may be "time to put the shoe on the other foot." As Mimi reminds us, "It's a poor rule that only works one way." You can do it. "Where there's a will, there's a way."

IV. TAKING CARE

of the

YOUNGER GENERATION

(Launching them on their road

to independence)

What Would Mimi Say

about

Taking Care of the Younger Generation?

❖ Nobody loves your kids like you do.

❖ You make one step; I'll help you make two.

❖ As children, they are tied to your apron strings; as adults, they are tied to your heart strings.

❖ Every tub's gotta stand on its own bottom.

❖ Learn to paddle your own canoe.

❖ Every goodbye is not gone. They sometimes come back.

Taking Care of the Younger Generation

You thought by this time in your life, your children would be gone and making it on their own - emotionally, physically and financially. Think again. They're not! In some cases, they're back; in others, they never left. Many are still in college; some have returned home after college; others just don't seem to be able to figure out how to survive independently. In any event, here you are back (or still) in the parenting role in a way you never envisioned you'd be at this age. But, the tugs on your heartstrings, coupled with a realistic view of their situation, combine to make you want to (or feel you must) help. Welcome, again, to the sandwich generation - those of you sandwiched between aging parents and adult (or minor) kids. Remember, Mimi said, "As children, they are tied to your apron strings; as adults, they are tied to your heart strings." As both, they may be tied to your purse strings.

I often tell my friends that Mimi had many titles in her lifetime - friend, neighbor, wife, sister, aunt, co-worker, boss - to name a few. But, the one she relished most was **Mother**! Her love for us was deep and abiding and, though my spouse and I have no children of our own, I see this same level of love and commitment in most of our friends and colleagues for their own offspring. They will always be parents willing to make sacrifices and to go to whatever lengths are required to ensure their children are safe, properly cared for, and always feel cared about. The bond between parent and child is unbreakable and their children have come to know them as a "safe place to land" when they are troubled or stressed and need guidance.

In the previous chapter, we discussed the many things you can consider to ease the path with regards to your aging parents - both for them and for you. In this chapter, we will work on the balancing act that you as a parent sometimes must perform between taking care of yourself and helping your children without jeopardizing your own financial future or making them feel like failures because they need help. Let's look at some of the issues related to dealing with your offspring, who I refer to as "the younger generation." They are the third leg of the stool; they are the other side of the sandwich.

Grown children who return home to live with their parents are sometimes referred to as "boomerang" children. In a recent College Board survey, almost half of the surveyed college graduates reported they planned to return home to their parents' nest to live for a while after college.

How do you begin to make the situation work with an adult child returning home and, at the same time manage your own stress level? While you want to be sensitive to their plight, in your continuing role as parent and teacher, you know you must give them the skills needed to eventually make it on their own.

First, let's talk about the background of this new family dynamic and how you fit into it. Then, we'll discuss what you might do to survive it and how to make it work for everyone.

The term "family dynamics" is defined as "the interactions between family members as well as the varying relationships that can exist within a family." Uncovering these relationships can help you to better understand your own family as well as others', including how families function. These dynamics are one part of a larger system defined by the individual members' relationships with each other. Families exist as their own structure made of people who share bonds and a sense of history and endeavor to meet each other's needs. Let's see how your desire to be a compassionate, helpful and responsive resource for your young adult loved one, coupled at times with your own inner struggle, fits into the discussion at hand.

According to data published by the U.S. Census Bureau, as recently as the 1990s, only 25% of young adults between ages 18 and 24 lived with their parents. By the year 2000, that number had more than doubled to 52% and continues to grow. The results of the Pew Research Center's 2012 survey show that " … almost half of adults in their 40s and 50s are either raising a young child or financially supporting a grown child (age 18 or older)." The reality is the financial burden on this group has grown dramatically and this increased pressure seems to be coming more from grown children than from aging parents.

What can you do going forward to help ensure that your children - both minors and adults - are equipped with the financial skills needed to guide them so they travel their paths to independence safely and knowledgeably? One way to begin this process is to insist they become financially literate, i.e., that they learn the rules of the money game and how to play it to win, starting at an early age. (You need to do for them what Mimi did for us - insist we not only learn the rules of the money game but also understand that, as we became adults, we would be responsible for our own financial well-being and for taking care of ourselves. We thought she was being mean and stingy. She told us she was teaching us lessons to last a lifetime. And, they have. We all know how to manage our money.)

As far as your children are concerned, they should understand that while help may come from others along the way, the primary responsibility for their well-being is theirs and theirs alone. Convey to them what Mimi told us more often than I can count, "Learn to paddle your own canoe;" and "Every tub's gotta stand on its own bottom." This may seem harsh and you may love them dearly, but you still have to prepare them for the day they will not have you to catch them if they fall.

There are several financial literacy programs that can help with the learning process. Programs may be offered in some schools, local libraries and community centers in your town. Also, they are offered through a variety of independent organizations including brokerage houses, financial planning firms, non-profits, estate planning attorneys' offices and real estate firms. (Some are listed in Appendix D along with programs aimed specifically at young kids.)

There is one independent program I know well and have taught numerous times for schools, civic organizations, churches, private firms and government institutions. The program is called **Camp Millionaire**. Offered in a camp-like setting, it teaches financial literacy to children (ages 9-12), teens (ages 13-17) and adults (18 and older) in a series of one- to five-day sessions, using age-appropriate language. It is high-spirited, gamey, and fun, with lots of laughter, class participation, competitions, and loads of prizes. At the end of the program, it is amazing how much knowledge has been transferred and how much the participants have learned about the rules of the money game. More information and scheduling for Camp Millionaire is available on the websites *www.creativewealthintl.org* or *www.yourmonmeywiz.com*.

Let's take another look at some of the Pew survey results. Almost 75% of the 2012 survey respondents with children over age 18 said they provided some financial support to at least one of them. More than 42% of these same survey respondents between ages 40 and 59 who have a grown child provided **primary** financial support. This is up significantly from the 33% who said they provided primary financial support in the 2005 survey. Even when the financial support was not considered primary, almost half of the respondents indicated they gave some type of financial aid in the previous year and felt it was their responsibility to do so.

A study by the National Endowment for Financial Education found that " ... more than 25% of parents surveyed took on additional debt to help their children and grandchildren. About 7% said they had to delay their retirement because of it.

Many members of the sandwich generation waited until later in life to become parents than earlier generations did. As a result, those of you who did are still raising minor children and having to pay all of the expenses associated with that. They are costs you expected to have to incur when you chose to become a parent. It's the adult children who you may have believed would be self-sufficient by now but aren't, who are the source of your inner struggle.

For the moment, let us assume your adult children are **not** being irresponsible when they say they need some financial support from you. They think the need is temporary and have come to you because you have always been there for them and they hope you will be, once again.

There are several reasons they might need your help or may need to return home. Here are a few:

- Many adult children are still (or again) enrolled in school full time and are not fully employed. Several professional degree/designation programs require additional training and, therefore, take longer than the standard four years to complete, e.g., medical school, law school, business school, and nursing school.

- The slow, uneven economic recovery of the past decade has had a disproportionate impact on young adults, making it harder for them to find jobs. Driven by a less-than-stellar job market, in 2010, the percentage of young adults employed was the lowest reported since the government started collecting this data in 1948.

- The continued drop in average weekly earnings for full-time employed young adults means they are making less than people in their age group have in the past and have fewer financial resources to work with.

- The level of student debt reached a staggering $1.2 trillion in March 2014. Many former students are facing loan repayment terms that are difficult for them to meet alone and deferment periods have elapsed with payments now due and payable.

- Many retirement-age workers are remaining in the workforce because they don't have enough retirement resources or because they feel "young" enough to keep working. In either event, the upshot is still the same. There are fewer jobs vacancies available to be filled.

- The high divorce rate (over 50% in 2010) has led some to have lower than expected financial resources to live on. Many former spouses are paying alimony and child support while trying to provide for their own separate living expenses. Others have to "make do" without the benefit of a second income.

- The need to save money for a house, business venture, travel, etc., has caused young adults to want to minimize current outlays, causing them to want to "temporarily" move back home.

- Legal problems might make it difficult for some to secure their own living space since a potential landlord or financial institution could be unwilling to contract with him/her, at least not without a co-signer - you!

- Unforeseen medical incidents or other health issues may have impacted his/her earnings stream.

What can you do to sensitively guide your child through this difficult financial period? Your ultimate goal is to teach them to make it on their own and become financially independent. But, you know it has to be done with care and compassion.

What are some steps you could take to help your young adult loved one get through a tough financial time?

In addition to understanding the emotional trauma he/she may be experiencing, you will need to educate yourself about your child's finances to determine the amount and timing of any financial support he/she may need. You will also want to know whether the money is needed to cover a short-term emergency, for ongoing expenses, to pay a particular bill, or for something else.

The clearest way to view your loved one's complete financial picture is to sit down with him/her and develop a realistic 6-to-12-month budget that includes all of the income and expenses he/she expects to have during the time period covered. Be prepared to find that when total outlays are deducted from anticipated income, there will be a shortfall. If not, there would be no need to come to you for help.

The most critical part of this exercise is to be certain that **all** expenses are included so the budget is complete. It does no good to include only those expenses he/she chooses to acknowledge. This budget should contain items that reflect whatever current reality he/she is living. Some of the expenses will exist if he/she lives in your home. Others will be added if he/she is living independently. So, you have to decide what living arrangement the two of you are budgeting for.

In addition to the numerical exercise of preparing a budget, you have to begin the conversations about the ultimate goal of having your child live on his/her own. You certainly can be an empathetic ear when it comes to his/her specific situation - job loss, divorce, economic downturn - but, there also should be a plan made with a realistic timetable that launches him/her on the path to independence. Otherwise, you may have an unplanned-for "roommate" for an extended period of time.

When one of my sisters decided not to go to college, Mimi told her she had to find a job right after graduating from high school. My sister asked where she would find one. Mimi gave a response that I will never forget. She said, "We live in the nation's capital. After you cross 1st Street Northwest, there is a government office building on every corner. I know you can find a job in one of them!"

After that, every morning, Mimi had my sister get up, get dressed and go into town when she and my Fther went to work. According to my sister, after they crossed 1st Street Northwest, she never knew at which red light my Mother would open the door and say, "OK, out!" Needless to say, my sister found a job in short order, ended up becoming a career civil servant, and retired from the federal government early. She learned to "paddle her own canoe."

Now, back to the budget we were talking about. A large part of your role as a parent has been to teach your children what they need to know to be self-sufficient. Terms like "sacrifice," "do it yourself," "do without" and "do it on a smaller scale" are important ones to bring up during this type of discussion. There may be things he/she would love to do but cannot, right now. There may be things he/she might like to have someone else do, but the funds aren't there, right now. This doesn't mean the child is a failure or that things may not be different in the future. You are just trying to help him/her realize that, right now, these changes are necessary for everybody to be able to get through this understandably difficult time.

You won't serve them well if you just do a budget for them and hand it over. You need to walk through this whole process with them, slowly explaining the components - what they are, why they are important, and the need to be as accurate as possible to end up with a meaningful, useful document he/she is willing to live with.

In the income section of the budget, all resources should be shown. These include things like:

- Wages – from full-time or part-time employment

- Bonuses

- Tax refunds

- Gifts

Then, we move to the expense section. Listed below are several types of expenses he/she may have. The expenses have been separated into two categories: 1) those that will be incurred if the young adult lives with you; and 2) those added expenses if he/she lives separately.

A. The budgeted expense categories for a young adult who **lives with you** may include:

- Rent - in whatever amount you have set. (You may consider allowing your child to live with you rent-free for a while. After that, you might insist they contribute something, even if you end up saving it for them until after they leave.)

- Student loan payments

- Credit card payments

- Auto-related expenses - car payment, gas, insurance, repairs, tags, license renewal

- Insurances - such as life, health, if they aren't still on your insurance, including an amount for co-pays, disability and long-term-care

- Cell phone

- Child care

- Clothing

- Laundry

- Gifts - including birthdays, anniversaries, holiday, graduation, etc. (should be minimal under the circumstances)

- Miscellaneous

B. Additional expenses if he/she **lives independently** may include:

- Mortgage/Rent payments - depending upon whether he/she is a homeowner or a renter

- Taxes

- Home maintenance - for homeowners

- Homeowner or renter's insurance

- Utilities - including water, gas/electric, home phone, cell phone, cable, burglar alarm, etc.

- Food

If, after projected expenses are subtracted from projected income, a deficit exists, then comes the hard part and you should expect some push-back. The two of you must look very carefully at each of the anticipated expenses to see which ones can be reduced or eliminated altogether or explore ways to increase income to make the budget balance. This is where the concept of needs versus wants becomes a reality. You may think obvious candidates for reduction will be items you deem to be non-essential - at least not at the proposed dollar level - such as clothing, entertainment, vacations, gifts and miscellaneous. Your child may disagree. If so, then look at the income side and see whether there are ways to increase the dollars coming in such as getting a second job or working overtime at his/her current job. In any event, at the end of the day, the budget has to balance.

Once "finalized," you should regularly review the budget with your child to determine if it represents his/her actual income and expense patterns, and the extent to which the plan is being followed.

If either of the above is not true, you will want to do several things:

- First, work with him/her to develop realistic adjustments.

- Second, try to figure out what can be done to get him/her to commit to following this important personal budget.

- Third, determine whether a different financial commitment from you is warranted and, if it is, how much and to what extent you are willing to make that commitment. As was true when trying to help aging parents, for you, an additional financial commitment may mean an adjustment to your own standard of living to provide the help needed.

This process of trying to help your young adult through a tough financial period can be emotionally and financially trying for all concerned. So, be careful. This is where the balancing act becomes crucial. You want to be helpful on the one hand, but, on the other hand, you can't do it at the expense of jeopardizing your own financial future.

> **What are some non-financial steps you might take to help a member of the "younger generation" prepare for a better financial future?**

Though not strictly financial in terms of current outlays, there are several other topics you should at least begin a discussion about. They may not represent immediate needs, but, given the uncertainty of life experiences we all face, planning and preparation can never start too soon. These include:

- The cost and feasibility of long-term-care insurance (if he/she doesn't have it already) to provide care in the event of a devastating illness or injury

- Existence of estate planning documents such as Wills/Trusts, Powers of Attorney and an Advance Medical Directive

- Selecting an executor/personal representative to handle estate planning needs

- Selecting a guardian (if there are minor children)

- Appropriateness of current beneficiary designations

To a young adult, these may seem like "just housekeeping matters" that won't be needed for some time. Given that we have no way of knowing when something may happen that will make us wish we had certain things in place, it is prudent to try to at least begin the dialogue about these matters. For example, long-term-care insurance is cheaper the younger one is when the policy is issued and premium increases rarely occur unless the insurance commission in the state in which the insured lives authorizes a premium increase on **all** policies. In addition, he/she should be reminded that "serious" medical conditions may make one ineligible for different kinds of life or long-term-care insurance. (As of 2014, the Affordable Care Act eliminated the disqualification due to pre-existing medical conditions.) Since one never knows when an accident may occur, it is best to take care of these matters while one is still healthy.

What are some other ways you can provide financial assistance to your offspring if they are in need?

Each year, *Kiplinger Magazine* reports several ways members of the sandwich generation can help their kids. Below are a few of the many tips the magazine has listed that you might consider as you ponder ways to assist them but still help them "grow up" and assume responsibility for themselves. (A few additional tips have been added by the author.)

- Make a **one-time**, lump sum gift of a certain amount that he/she will be required to budget, as opposed to paying his/her expenses directly. The idea behind this is that doing so will force him/her to have to allocate the dollars carefully since you have said this is a one-shot deal. The challenge for you will be to stick to your guns if he/she asks for more.

- Help pay a few very important bills if you don't have a lump sum of money you are able or willing to give. Examples are expenses like car payment, student loan payment, insurances and rent. This way, you know these expenses are being paid. If this really is your limit, then, you have to be prepared to say so no matter what the reason is more is needed.

- Consider having your child sign a long-term promissory note in an amount sufficient to pay off (or at least substantially pay down) some of his/her high-cost debt. At some time in the future, you may choose to make a gift of part of or the entire loan depending upon your own then-current and anticipated financial needs.

- If your child is college age, try to interest him/her in a nearby junior college to cut back on overall college expenses. Work with him/her to choose one that has both excellent transfer and academic records.

- If your child is under age 26 and loses his/her job, consider having him/her covered by your health insurance policy. This may be cheaper than having him/her pay for coverage through his/her prior employer's COBRA, plan which allows a continuation of benefits under the old group plan for a limited amount of time if the insured pays up to 102% of the plan's cost. COBRA is usually a very expensive alternative.

- Investigate adding him/her to your auto insurance/health policies and cell phone plan to see whether this is more cost-effective than having his/her own coverage.

What are non-financial ways you can help your kids if they are having financial difficulties?

There are non-financial tips and suggestions you might make that your loved ones can implement to ease their financial burden. Some of them might include the following:

- Introduce them to comparison and coupon websites such as *www.ebizmba.com/articles/coupon-websites.*

- Advise them to become a better cook to save money by cutting down on the high cost of eating out.

- Suggest they consider part-time employment of some sort until they can find the full-time job they want. This will provide some income, which is better than none. Even if they are already employed part-time, if their expenses exceed their income, then another part-time job may be necessary, at least until they can find full-time employment that pays enough to cover their expenses.

- If he/she is a homeowner, suggest trying to reduce utility bills through things like proper insulation, programmable thermostats and participating in a free time-of-use service offered by the local utility company.

- Ask him/her to think about whether he/she has or can develop an income-producing sellable skill. Eventually, this might even turn into a serious business and become a major source of income.

- Suggest that he/she give more thoughtful, less expensive and more creative gifts. Often, these are more appreciated and more valued by the recipient than an expensive, common, store-bought gift.

- Have him/her consider doing what he/she pays others to do. Things like housecleaning, yard maintenance, car washing and cooking (versus eating out) immediately come to mind as examples.

While some of these suggestions may seem a bit harsh, the intent is that you want to be helpful but also want to continue parenting and providing guidance. You, alone, cannot solve the problem. But, you do want to shine a light on the path that leads to self-sufficiency.

If your child has college debt, what can be done to help ease that burden?

The high cost of college has exacted a tremendous toll on our nation's young people. At the end of the first quarter of 2014, according to Edvisors.com, 4.1 million borrowers (federal and private loans combined) owed a staggering $1.2 trillion! They also report that defaults on student loans are rising at an alarming rate.

Re-paying student loans is a burden for many borrowers. According to the Department of Education, student loan debt losses continue to mount each day as more and more borrowers fall behind on their payments. Almost 10% of the more than 4.0 million federal student loan borrowers who began paying back their loans in the 2011 fiscal year had defaulted by the end of the next fiscal year. That was the sixth consecutive year of documented rising defaults. College graduates who default on their student debt loan payments may damage their credit; have wages garnished; and/or see their tax refunds taken by Uncle Sam.

It isn't just former students who are saddled with this debt. More and more parents and grandparents have co-signed on loans to help pay for their young adult loved ones' college education. These co-signers end up on the hook if their children/grandchildren are unable to (or refuse to) repay the loans. According to Measure One, the most recognized source for student loan data and analysis, almost 80% of the private loans that were refinanced or consolidated by the seven largest lenders in the 2012-2013 academic year had co-signers, most often parents of the student borrower.

According to the General Accounting Office, federal student debt for those in the 65-74 age bracket increased from $2.8 billion in 2005 to $18.2 billion in 2013. This debt is split about 50/50 between sandwich generation-ers own debt and that of their children and grandchildren for whom they had co-signed. Another sobering fact is that this age group is also defaulting on its student loans in record numbers.

There are several ways to lighten the debt load:

1. **To make your loved one's student loan debt more manageable by reducing the monthly payment amount, look into one of the federal-government-mandated, income-driven repayment plans.** These plans set the required monthly payment as a percentage of the borrower's discretionary income, as opposed to their debt load and the date of the loans. Such a plan may be applicable if the borrower's outstanding federal student loan debt is higher than or is a significant portion of his/her annual income.

   There are three different types of these plans and most **federal** student loans are eligible for at least one of them. They have different eligibility requirements, payment amounts and payback periods. At least one of them, the

IBR Plan described below, has a loan forgiveness component. The plans are:

A. Income-Based Repayment Plan (IBR Plan)

B. Pay As You Earn Repayment Plan (Pay As You Earn Plan)

C. Income-Contingent Repayment Plan (ICR Plan)

The following chart shows how payment amounts are determined under each income-driven plan. Depending on your income and family size, you may have no monthly payment at all.

Income-Driven Repayment Plan	Payment Amount
IBR Plan for those who are not new borrowers on or after July 1, 2014	Generally 15% of your discretionary income, but never more than the 10-year Standard Repayment Plan amount. The repayment period is 25 years.
IBR Plan for those who are new borrowers on or after July 1, 2014	Generally 10%of your discretionary income, but never more than the 10-year Standard Repayment Plan amount. The repayment period is 20 years.
Pay As You Earn Plan	Generally 10% of your discretionary income, but never more than the 10-year Standard Repayment Plan amount. The repayment period is 20 years.
ICR Plan	The lesser of the following: • 20% of your discretionary income;

or

- The amount you would pay on a repayment plan with a fixed payment over the course of 12 years, adjusted according to your income. The repayment period is 25 years.

For more information and to determine which plan works best for you and your loved one's situation, go to the Department of Education's Student Aid website at *www.studentaid.ed.gov/repay-loans/understand/plans/income-driven*.

2. **To actually get rid of some of their student debt, see whether your borrower qualifies for one of the student loan forgiveness programs.** The Student Loan Forgiveness Act, passed in 2012, provides several ways borrowers can have their federal student loans **forgiven** through a variety of government programs. At the end of the day, in some programs, borrowers end up debt free! Below are the four ways of partial or complete loan forgiveness allowed by the Act.

- **Become a public school teacher in a low-income area.**

   Under the government's **Teacher Forgiveness Program**, up to $17,500 of a student's federal Stafford loans or all of their Perkins loans can be forgiven in exchange for five consecutive, full-time years as a teacher at certain low-income elementary or secondary schools.

- **Join the military.**

  Each branch of the military has its own student loan forgiveness program. Forgiven loan amounts usually depend on the level of rank achieved. Before signing up, the borrower should contact their preferred branch to learn about how that branch's program works.

- **Participate in the Income-Based Repayment Plan (IBR) described above.**

  The IBR adjusts students' monthly loan payments to be no more than 15% of their "discretionary" income (the amount of money they make that falls above the federal poverty level). After 25 years of making these adjusted loan payments, the borrower's remaining balance is completely forgiven.

  For example, suppose a recent graduate makes $20,000 annually. Because the federal poverty level within the contiguous U.S. is $11,490 for 2014, that means he only makes $8,510 in discretionary income. Under the IBR, he would only have to make payments that were 15% of that $8,510, which equals about $106 a month. (It's possible that some recent graduates make so little they qualify to make no payments.)

- **Get a public service, government or non-profit job.**

  Those who borrowed money under the William D. Ford Federal Direct Loan Program can apply to the **Public Service Loan Forgiveness Program**. In this program, full-time employees in the public service or non-profit sectors can have the remainder of their outstanding debt forgiven after they successfully make 120 qualified loan payments.

What kinds of jobs qualify as public service? Any employment with a federal, state or local government agency, entity or organization, or a 501C (3) not-for-profit organization qualifies.

Not long ago, I counseled a 28-year-old single female who is a medical doctor about to complete a fellowship program. She was trying to determine which of two employment opportunities to take. One was a two-year assignment with the United Nations (U.N.) in South Africa; the other was what she considered her ideal job - doing research with a major New York university. When she told me she had more than $200,000 in outstanding student debt that would be wiped out if she took the U.N. job, to me, the choice was a no-brainer! I was being very candid with her when I told her that if she ever wanted to get married, she was a basic "bad risk" with a $200,000 bogey over her head and that she should take the U.N. job.

Her story has a fairytale ending. She took the U.N. job; met her prospective spouse on the plane on the way to South Africa; completed her two year stint; returned to New York; married him; got her research job; and now lives happily with him and their young daughter in New York.

In return for volunteer service, AmeriCorps provides funds to repay student loan debts and the Peace Corps offers partial debt cancellation. Similarly, the Nurse Corps Loan Repayment Program allows nurses working in "critical-shortage facilities" to pay off up to 60% of nursing school loans. These are all viable options for students with limited resources and large debts.

3. **Consolidate all the student loans into one loan with a fixed interest rate.** That way, rather than making several payments each month - a separate one for each loan - borrowers can make one payment and only have a single loan servicer to deal with. That alone can result in lower payments. (Federal and private loans shouldn't be consolidated because private lenders don't have all of the repayment options permitted by federal loans.)

4. **Try to refinance outstanding loans to get a lower rate.**

5. **For federal loans, if they have been consolidated, extend the repayment period from the standard 10 years up to the maximum allowable 30 years, depending upon the amount of debt owed.** Borrowers who owe at least $20,000 can extend their payments to 20 years whereas those who owe at least $60,000 can extend the repayment period up to 30 years. Understand that with the extension, although the monthly payments are lower, the total amount of interest paid will be greater even though the rate remains the same.

6. **If federal loans have not been consolidated and the outstanding debt exceeds $30,000, extend the repayment period to 25 years.** Again, with the extension, the monthly payments will be lower but, even with no change in the interest rate, the total amount of interest paid will be significantly greater.

7. **Try to negotiate a longer repayment period if there are any private loans.** The repayment periods on private loans vary

from 5 to 15 years, depending upon the lender. Private lenders are under no obligation to renegotiate their loan terms.

The Consumer Financial Protection Bureau has created a "pay student debt" tool at *www.consumerfinance.gov* to help borrowers understand repayment choices. It also shows various ways to capitalize on debt relief plans.

The objectives of this chapter have been fourfold:

1. To help you understand, from a statistical and economic point of view, why your adult child might need your financial assistance at this point in his/her life;

2. To give you the tools needed to help guide him/her through a difficult financial transition period. (Mimi said, "You make one step, I'll help you make two.")

3. To familiarize you with ways to help your young adult become critically aware of his/her current financial situation; and

4. To provide tools and information to help your loved one be able to set out on (or return to) a path of financial independence.

With the information contained here, the hope is your loved ones will be able to go forward more informed, more focused and more determined to take care of themselves and will be launched on their road to independence. That would be the best possible outcome for everyone involved.

V. RETIREMENT SECRETS

the

SANDWICH GENERATION

SHOULD KNOW

(Easing through your "Golden Years")

What Would Mimi Say

about

Retirement?

❖ God bless the "child" who's got his own.

❖ Every tub's gotta stand on its own bottom.

❖ You work hard, then you get to play hard.

Retirement Secrets the
Sandwich Generation Should Know

According to the results of a 2014 survey conducted by Bankrate.com, " ... a lot of people have empty nest eggs. In fact, more than a third of Americans (36%) have nothing saved for retirement. When dissecting the numbers into various age groups, they are equally as startling. 14% of people 65 and older have no retirement savings; 26% of those ages 50 to 64 have nothing saved; 33% of those ages 30 to 49 and 69% of those ages 18 to 29 have not put anything aside for their retirement."

The results of a 2013 telephone survey of 1,000 workers from the non-profit Employee Benefit Research Institute and Greenwald and Associates showed that many people aren't saving nearly enough for their golden years. About 36% of workers had less than $1,000 in savings and investments that could be used for retirement, not counting their primary residence or retirement plans. Almost 60% had less than $25,000.

At a reception a couple of years ago, I met a 49-year-old federal employee. When she found out that I teach financial education and even had taught classes at her agency, she asked for some advice. It turned out she had absolutely nothing saved for retirement and wanted to retire in 6 years at age 55, which the federal government permits and considers full retirement as long as you have 30 years of service. (Her federal retirement would be minimal since she had not even participated in the Thrift Savings Plan (TSP), the federal equivalent of the 401(k). She told me she had been a compulsive spender and saving money had not been a priority until recently.

She looked like all the air had been let out of her balloon when I told her she could not get there from here. It is numerically impossible, even if she saved every after-tax dollar of her $90,000 annual salary, for her to put aside, in 6 years, enough to cover 25 years or so of post-retirement expenses. Yes, she should save every penny she can for retirement, but it is not likely to be enough for her to live off of without significantly lowering her living standards in retirement or getting another job. Another option, and the one that is most likely, is that she delay her retirement for many years.

As you can see from the statistics above and the example I cited, many people are not saving for retirement. And, in many cases, even if they are saving, it is not nearly enough to finance the retirement lifestyle they hope to live. This is not a club you want to proudly join.

For those who want the information needed to ensure a comfortable, well-planned retirement, following is a discussion of topics and answers to pertinent questions which should help make that happen.

> **What should I be doing now to make sure I have enough money to live the life I want in retirement?**

You may have a very idealistic vision of retirement - doing all of the things that you never seem to have time to do now – traveling; going to exotic places; visiting friends; learning a new language; enrolling in cooking school; doing nothing, etc. How do you make that vision, whatever it is for you, a reality?

First and foremost, you must make saving for retirement a priority. Here are a few tips.

1. Start saving now, if you haven't already!

2. Save regularly!

3. Save as much as you can - at least enough to maximize employer contributions!

4. Don't dip into your retirement savings!

Many people I've talked to over the years regret their lack of retirement planning and wish they had gotten more financial education and advice during their younger years, similar to what Mimi gave us. Most wished for a "do over," but, we know that's not possible. Don't despair; hope is not lost. Retirement planning is not as complicated as it once was, thanks to many tools and resources available both in print and on the internet.

The one thing you don't want to do is outlive your financial resources. You want to be able to fund and afford your retirement so you can comfortably live the lifestyle you want, or you may have to adjust your expectations or delay retirement. Following are some basic steps to get you started.

You have to figure out:

1. How much money you will need, annually, to pay for the lifestyle you want

2. The age at which you want to retire

3. The amount you already have saved for retirement

4. For planning purposes, the number of years you expect to live in retirement

5. The average return on investments you expect to earn

With values for each of these elements, you and your advisers will be able to determine how much you need to save (to cover the gap between what you have today and what you will need at retirement) during each of your remaining working years to put together a pot of dollars sufficient to fund your golden years. There are several retirement calculators on the web at sites such as *www.schwab.com*; *www.fidelity.com*; *and www.ubs.com*. (See example in Appendix B and other retirement calculation sites listed in Appendix D.)

More specifically, following are the steps you need to take:

- **Determine your retirement income needs:**

  To determine your specific needs, you first need to estimate your annual retirement expenses using your current expenses as a guide. (Your expenses may be very different by the time you retire.) If you're nearing retirement, the difference between your current expenses and your retirement expenses may be small. If retirement is many years away, the difference may be significant and projecting your future expenses may be more challenging. But, do the best you can.

  Remember to take inflation into account. According to 2012 U.S. Department of Labor statistics, the average annual rate of inflation over the past 20 years has been approximately 2.4%. So, expect your expenses to rise annually by at least the average inflation rate.

  Keep in mind that your annual expenses may vary throughout retirement. For example, if you are a homeowner with a mortgage when you retire, your housing expenses will be lower once the mortgage is paid off. However, taxes, insurance and household repairs still have to be paid with the latter possibly being higher than today, given that the house is aging. Some other expenses, especially medical, also may increase as you age. The main thing to remember is to revisit your estimated income and expenses regularly to reaffirm they reflect your latest experience.

- **Calculate your funding gap:**

  Once you have estimated your retirement income needs, it's time to look at the income you expect to receive in retirement. Your income may come from a variety of sources such as Social Security, a pension plan at work, a part-time job and/or investments. If estimates show that your future assets and income will fall short of what you need to cover your projected expenses, that gap has to come from personal savings, a fairy godMother, or another full- or part-time job. The funding gap represents the amount you need to save to fund the retirement you say you want.

- **Build a retirement fund to fill the gap. Save, save, save!**

  When you know, roughly, how much money you'll need, your next goal is to save that amount by the time you retire. First, you'll have to map out a savings plan that works for you. Assume a conservative rate of return, and then determine about how much you'll need to save every month/year between now and your retirement to reach your goal.

  The next step is to put your savings plan into action. If possible, fund your retirement plan through payroll deductions and have the funds automatically invested in the programs of your choice, e.g., 401(k), 403(b), employee stock purchase plan or other savings. Funding using automatic payroll deductions reduces the temptation to not follow your plan.

- **Understand your investment options**

Understand the types of investments that are available, and decide which ones are right for you. If you don't have the time, energy, education or inclination to do this yourself, hire a financial professional. He/she will explain the options that are available to you and will help you to select investments that are appropriate for your goals, risk tolerance and timeframe..

The most important thing for you to do is to put a plan into motion as soon as possible. You need to monitor your progress regularly and make needed adjustments as your situation changes. Remember, saving for your own retirement is your responsibility and yours alone. Continue to educate yourself about managing your money and investing and get professional help if you don't think you have the knowledge and/or time to go it alone. No matter how old you are, it's never too early or too late to save for your tomorrow.

Several years ago, I had a 53 year-old participant in one of my federal government classes who definitely did not prioritize saving for retirement, despite the fact that she was a federal employee, had several investment options open to her and would even get a match on her savings up to the plan's specified maximum percentage.

Why was she not saving for her retirement the way she knew she should? The reason was that she had a 25-year-old son who wouldn't work and wouldn't move! She and her spouse literally paid all of his expenses - car, gas, insurance, clothing and entertainment. He had graduated from college at age 24, tried working for a year, didn't like it and quit his job. So, she couldn't put money aside for her retirement because she was spending so much on him.

I candidly told her that not only was she crippling him, but also, when she got older and needed money, she would not have the resources she needed and probably would not find a reputable institution that would give her a loan. She does not want to be the burden on him that he is on her today. (Mimi would have said, "I know I taught you better than that!")

This is the kind of situation I want all of you to avoid at all costs. Go back to the beginning of the book where one of the early chapters talks about taking care of yourself first. This story I just shared with you is a classic example of someone making bad decisions that may come back to haunt her. Don't let it happen to you!

When should I start taking my Social Security benefits?

You can begin receiving Social Security retirement benefits as early as age 62. However, your benefit may be 25% to 30% less than if you wait until your full retirement age (currently 66 or 67, depending on the year you were born). The amount by which your benefit will permanently decrease depends upon how close you are to full retirement age when you start to take those benefits. But, you also collect them longer than if you had waited until full retirement age.

You can wait until **after** your full retirement age to start taking benefits. According to actuaries at the Social Security Administration, only about 5% of retirees wait until **after** they've actually reached full retirement age to begin collecting benefits. And, they say, it's a trend that's likely to continue. Those who do wait enjoy about an 8% annual increase in future benefits until they reach age 70. Then, there is no further benefit increase, so, there is no advantage to any delay.

"Retirees who file for Social Security at age 62 and live into their mid-90s could lose as much as $150,000 in benefits," due to the permanent lower monthly benefit they will receive, according to Ron Gebhardsbauer, senior pension fellow with the American Academy of Actuaries. The loss could be greater if you factor in inflation. The U.S. Census Bureau reports that today, there is at least a 41% chance a 62- year-old woman will live to be 90. A 62-year-old man has almost a 30% chance.

According to the Social Security Administration, the average retiree's "break even" age for Social Security benefits is 77. A retiree who dies before then would have fared better by taking benefits at age 62. (The "break-even age" is the age at which the total of your early retirement benefits no longer exceeds the amount you would have collected if you waited until your full retirement age.) If you think you'll live past your "break-even age," it may pay to wait until full retirement age or perhaps even longer (up to age 70) to start collecting your benefits.

Another factor to consider in the decision about when to start receiving your benefits is whether you plan to continue to work after age 62. Under current law, beneficiaries who haven't reached their full retirement age are subject to an "earnings test." That test reduces your benefits by $1 for every $2 you earn, up to the annual limit. (In 2014, the limit is $15,480.) Your benefit will be increased at your full retirement age to account for benefits withheld due to earlier earnings.

These statistics may not matter much, depending upon your particular situation. For those in poor health, who have lost loved ones prematurely, who would be taxed highly on the benefit received, or who have been forced into early retirement, to quote one of Mimi's favorite sayings, "A bird in the hand is worth two in the bush." It's a chance many are willing to take. The choice is yours to make.

How will retirement affect my IRAs and employer retirement plans?

The longer you delay retirement, the longer you can build up tax-deferred funds in your IRAs. (You must be receiving wages to contribute to an IRA.) If you delay retirement, you will also have a longer time to contribute to any employer-sponsored plans like a 401(k) or 403(b), and to receive any employer match.

By law, you are always 100% vested in your own contributions. On the other hand, when it comes to the employer match you may receive, the same is not true. (Vesting refers to the part of ownership that has been given to you by your employer.) Vesting schedules may be as generous as immediate vesting upon joining the company. More often, employees become vested based upon a pre-determined schedule and it is done over a number of years. If you retire before you are fully vested, you may forfeit some or all of any employer contributions. Be sure you understand your employer's vesting schedule to maximize your opportunity to get credit for their contributions. (By law, you must be fully vested after spending six years with any company.)

Will I need to buy health insurance after I retire?

Medicare doesn't start until you reach age 65. Does your employer provide post-retirement medical benefits? Are you eligible for the coverage if you retire early? If the answer to both of these questions is no, and you are under 65, you may have to look into COBRA (a self-paid continuation of your employer-subsidized medical plan that is generally allowed for up to 18 months) or a private individual policy, either of which could be very expensive. To protect yourself, your family and your assets, you should have medical coverage of some type.

In 2014, the Affordable Care Act became the law of the land. It provides insurance coverage for Americans under 65 who would not otherwise have affordable insurance coverage. However, it is not available to seniors 65 and older because seniors have access to Medicare, another government-sponsored program. There is no qualification requirement for Medicare, other than age.

Every year, Fidelity Investments releases the results of its latest estimate of medical expenses for retirees who do not have employer-provided retiree health-care coverage. For couples retiring in 2013, Fidelity estimates that a typical couple 65 years old will need $220,000 to cover medical expenses if the husband lives to age 82 and the wife to age 85. (This number includes costs related to Medicare Parts A, B and D. It does not, however, include over-the-counter medications, long-term care costs and dental.)

For many Americans, health care is likely to be one of their largest expenses in retirement. Fidelity cautions that " ... While some

Americans will have employer-sponsored retiree health benefits to help cover these expenses, the majority of Americans will need to plan to cover health care costs as part of their overall retirement savings strategy... It is extremely important to do so to ensure that retirees are prepared to pay their medical bills throughout retirement."

Is phasing into retirement sensible?

Retirement does not have to be an all-or-nothing proposition. If you're not quite ready for full retirement, financially or psychologically, consider lightening your workload and switching from full-time to part-time employment. This will allow you not only to continue to have an income source, but also remain active and productive.

Consider, for a Moment, my client who had a knack for baking. For many years after her early retirement, she baked and sold beautifully-decorated, tasty cakes. They were the talk of the town. Not only did this allow her to stay active on her own schedule, but also it provided her with supplemental income. At some point, she decided she didn't want to do that anymore and stopped, but on her own terms.

Should I contribute to the 401(k) or equivalent plan my employer offers?

Yes! You definitely should contribute to your employer's tax-free plan, unless you absolutely cannot afford to set aside anything at all. Such plans are, without a doubt, some of the most powerful tools you can use to save for retirement.

The first benefit is that your contributions to a 401(k) or equivalent plan are not taxed as current income. They come right off the top of your salary before taxes are withheld. This reduces your taxable income, allowing you to pay less in taxes each year. You eventually pay taxes on amounts contributed when you withdraw money from the plan, but you may be in a lower tax bracket by then.

Furthermore, money held in these plans grows tax deferred. The investment earnings on plan assets are not taxed as long as they remain inside the plan. Only when you withdraw those earnings will you pay taxes on them (again, possibly at a lower rate). In the meantime, tax-deferred growth gives you the opportunity to build a substantial balance over the long term, depending on your investments' performances.

If you're lucky, your employer matches your contributions up to a certain level, e.g., 50 cents on the dollar up to 6% of your salary. You typically become vested in your employer's contributions and related earnings through years of service. The details depend on the plan. Employer contributions are also pre-tax and are basically free money (once you're vested), so you should try to take full advantage of them. If you fail to make contributions and, thus, receive no match, you are leaving money on the table and are actually walking away from money your employer offers to you.

Finally, 401(k)s and their equivalents are a very convenient way to save. You decide what percentage of your salary to contribute, up to allowable limits, and your contributions are deducted automatically from your salary each pay period. Because the money never passes through your hands, there's no temptation to spend it or skip a contribution here and there. Also, just as there is

FDIC protection for financial institution deposits, ERISA (Employee Retirement Income Security Act of 1974) governs a private industry employer's use of your funds and protects the interests of employee benefit plan participants. Among other things, it requires that funds deposited through the plan be segregated from employer funds. It essentially provides protection for your money, even if the company ceases to exist or goes bankrupt.

Assuming I do save for retirement, how much of my savings can I withdraw each year and have it last for the rest of my life?

This is a topic where there is much debate and disagreement among financial professionals. The recommendations run from a low of 2.5% to a high of 4.5% (pre-tax), depending on the composition of your portfolio and your expected longevity, post retirement. The guideline that was developed more than 20 years ago is 4% the first year, plus an annual increase for inflation. According to Jane Bryant Quinn, a personal finance expert, the 4% guideline " ... would have carried retirees successfully through the worst 30-year period of the 20th century, including the periods starting in 1929 (recession) and 1973 (stagflation). It's too early to know the 30-year outcome for people who retired in 2000, but, according to Bill Bengen, the financial planner who developed the standard, the rule is working so far."

Some investment experts suggest that the more of your portfolio you have invested in stocks versus fixed income instruments like bonds, the higher the percentage you should be able to withdraw safely. (The 4% standard assumes you split your portfolio evenly between the two.) The lower-end withdrawal percentage of 2.5%

assumes your portfolio consists almost entirely of fixed-income instruments.

This is truly a decision you shouldn't make alone. There are professionals who work with clients daily on this type of decision. However, whatever percentage of your retirement savings you start off taking, it is imperative you and your investment advisers regularly revisit that decision to make sure you are neither taking out too much, thereby putting yourself in danger of running out of money prematurely; nor taking out too little, depriving yourself of enjoying the resources you have amassed. If you find you are taking out either too much or too little, then make the appropriate adjustment and enjoy the ride.

The tips provided here are to help you calculate and manage your retirement assets well. Though tedious, it is critical that you, along with the help of your advisers, ensure you do not outlive your money. Along the way, keep saving and keep rebalancing your portfolio so it always keeps pace with and reflects the retirement lifestyle you envision for yourself.

VI. LONG-TERM CARE GIVING

(Taking care of loved ones
who can't take care of themselves)

by

Jacqueline D. Byrd

Elder Care Attorney

www.byrdandbyrd.com

with

Patricia A. Davis

Financial Counselor and Author

www.yourmoneywiz.com

What Would Mimi Say

about

Long-term Care Giving?

❖ *One good turn deserves another.*

❖ *It's a poor rule that only works one way.*

❖ *Where there's a will, there's a way.*

❖ *God grant me the serenity to accept the things I cannot change, the courage to change the things I can and the wisdom to know the difference.*

❖ *No man is an island.* (You have to be willing to help those in need.)

Long-term Care Giving

If you are caring for a parent or other loved one, the first thing to know is that you are not alone. There is a wealth of available resources to help you.

Remember, the most effective planning is undertaken before a crisis. Ask yourself whether you and your loved ones are sufficiently knowledgeable about public and private community services. Do you feel you have the information needed to decide among home care, assisted living, continuing care retirement communities or nursing facility care options? Do you understand the differences between Medicare and Medicaid programs and their relevance to your family's plans? Are you aware of long-term-care insurance and what to look for in selecting an agent and a policy? Are you familiar with your asset protection options if someone needs long-term care or nursing-facility care?

Caregivers, be proud of yourselves. You are demonstrating that the words of love you have professed over the years are honest and true. You are showing your devotion in an extremely caring and meaningful way.

The field of caring for seniors is vast. It covers everything from health care, estate planning, housing, selecting caregivers, caregiver rights, insurance, and much more. In this chapter, Ms. Byrd and I will describe three of them:

1. Having "the talk" with your parents;

2. Factors to consider when choosing a nursing home; and

3. Issues around preparing for the cost of long-term care.

We hope the information contained here will help you better deal with these issues if and when you have to.

Thinking and Talking About Parents' Legal and Financial Affairs, i.e., Having "The Talk"

by

Jacqueline D. Byrd

If you're a baby boomer, you probably have already had the "birds and bees" talks with all your growing/grown children. But, have you had "the talk" with your aging parents, also?

That talk involves a frank discussion with parents about arrangements for the latter years of their life. The discussion should include, at a minimum, where your parents want to live, how they want to be cared for, how they want their money managed, and what kinds of burial or funeral arrangements they want.

The start of a new year can be a great time to begin thinking about parents' financial affairs and arrangements for the future though, any time is better than never. When the parents, for whatever reason, lose legal capacity to make important decisions, it is often too late to try to make satisfactory arrangements or good decisions. Certainly, at that point, they are in no position to provide input that lets you know what they want to do.

The hard part about talking with aging parents is that they're used to being in charge, instead of getting advice from their children. "It's one of the hardest things that we, as adult children, have to do," says Sandra Timmermann, a gerontologist and director of the

MetLife Mature Market Institute. "We have to be brave and take a deep breath and plunge into the cold water."

Harry S. Margolis, *ElderLawAnswers* founder and president, recently answered some questions for an article on talking with aging parents or other family members about sensitive issues. Below are some of the reporter's questions and Mr. Margolis' answers. Even if you are not facing these particular issues today, you might be sometime in the not-so-distant future, or have a close friend or relative who is. So, you might find this information instructive and helpful.

1. Q. At what point is it appropriate for grown children, spouses, caregivers or friends to try to discuss legal and financial issues with aging parents, relatives or friends?

   A. The earlier the better, but every family is different, and raising these issues can be more or less uncomfortable depending on family dynamics. Certainly, if there is an illness or medical emergency, that can serve as justification for beginning the discussion.

2. Q. What's the best way to broach the subject?

   A. Rather than focusing on the parent or other family member's current or possible future physical and mental decline, it often works better for the person starting the conversation to focus on his or her own concerns. She can say she was meeting with her own estate planning attorney, which made her think about her parents' situation. Or, she can talk about how she is nervous about being able to care for her parents if and when the need comes up. Often, parents won't take measures to protect themselves, but they never stop being parents and will respond to a call for help from a child.

3. Q. Where's the best place to have such a discussion?

    A. In the parent's home.

4. Q. Should you seek legal counsel before initiating a talk?

    A. Not necessarily. A legal consultation would help the children or other family members know what issues to discuss and some of the available options. But, the ultimate goal should be for the elder himself or herself to consult with an attorney with elder law experience. To the extent necessary, a family member should be there to help the elder with both communication and understanding of what's going on.

5. Q. Should it be one-on-one or should family members, friends or those with specific expertise in an area be part of the discussion?

    A. That has to be determined on a case-by-case basis. We always encourage transparency so that all family members are in the loop. However, scheduling can be difficult and too many people involved can be overwhelming. In addition, depending on the circumstances, elder care and planning issues can take several meetings to resolve. Different people may be involved in different meetings, depending on the issues being discussed at each.

6. Q. What if your parent/spouse/relative refuses to talk about these issues? How do you overcome this?

    A. Follow the advice above. If it's a parent, the "child" may have to be patient and wait until an opportunity arises to bring the subject up again. In the end, it may be impossible to get the parent to participate in any planning. If that happens, then there is nothing that can be done until it becomes clear the parent needs some sort of help. Then, a court-ordered intervention may become necessary. If it's a spouse who is resistant, this may also be true. However, a spouse may be able to take some planning steps on his or her own without the assistance or approval of the ailing spouse.

7. Q. What steps can you legally take to prevent an elderly person from driving, if they refuse to hand over their license or keys?

   A. This depends on the state. In some states, there are provisions for letting the registry of motor vehicles know of problem drivers. When family pressure doesn't stop a senior from driving and dementia exists, some of our clients have been successful in disabling vehicles if the senior does not have the capacity to get it fixed.

8. Q. What steps can you legally take if an elderly person such as a parent or spouse refuses to take care of issues dealing with a Will, housing, medical treatment or related areas?

   A. It depends on the parent or spouse's mental capacity. If they are incompetent, it is possible to go to court to be appointed guardian and to take over decision-making in these areas. Unfortunately, this can be an expensive, time-consuming and cumbersome process.

9. Q. What can seniors do, in advance, to avoid becoming embroiled with grown children, relatives, or friends over these issues?

   A. Seniors can plan ahead. All seniors should sit down with an elder law attorney to discuss their goals, concerns and hopes and to develop a plan to reach the goals, address the concerns and give their hopes the opportunity to become realities. At the same time, an elder law attorney should be engaged to complete any estate planning documents missing from the senior's arsenal, and to review all existing documents for completeness and to ensure they reflect the senior's then-current attitudes.

Hopefully, armed with the answers Mr. Margolis gave to the questions above, you can make having "the talk" a little easier and more productive for you and for your loved ones.

Factors to Consider When Choosing a Nursing Home
by

Jacqueline D. Byrd

If you are the caregiver for a loved one, one of the many perplexing questions is, "When is the right time to move to nursing home care?" What may seem like a simple question is actually part of an excruciating matter for everyone concerned. To the loved one who is ill, the right time may be never. On a very frustrating day for the caregiver, the right time may be this very minute. Is there, in fact, a right time? And when it comes, how do you go about selecting a facility that is "just right" for your loved one?

Choosing a nursing home for someone we love is one of the most heart-wrenching things that life can require of us. It is, without question, everybody's absolute last choice for themselves or their loved ones. Although there are more options than ever before, nursing homes remain the facilities that care for most of us as we continue to age. Nursing homes usher many of us to the edge of "that good night" into which Dylan Thomas urged us not to go gently.

Nursing facility care has radically improved since 1986 when the National Academy of Sciences published a report calling nursing homes "warehouses" for the elderly. The report criticized existing nursing home law, saying it focused on the capacity of each facility to provide services rather than on the quality of the services received by the residents. That is, the focus was on mechanical aspects of nursing homes such as square footage, staffing numbers, kinds of equipment and payments.

Congress responded to that report with the Federal Nursing Home Reform Act of 1987. The act was intended to focus on individual residents' needs - ensuring that residents are treated as people rather than as "units of reimbursement."

Family members usually are distraught, stressed and feel guilty when admitting another family member to a nursing home. Unfortunately, during what is usually a hasty admission procedure, it is possible to make costly mistakes and errors.

According to the website *www.medicare.gov*, your steps in choosing the right nursing home for you or your loved one will be to:

1. Identify nursing homes in your area

2. Compare the quality of the nursing homes you're considering

3. Visit the nursing homes that interest you, and

4. Make a choice.

The first step in the process is to identify all of the nursing homes in the area where your loved one will live. How can you do that?

- First, consult the free publication, *Sourcebook - Guide to Retirement Living.* This publication shows charts comparing area nursing homes according to services, and provides cost figures, ranging from lowest to highest. For a free copy, you can call the order line at 1-800-394-9990, Ext. 1126.

- Next, ask family, friends or acquaintances for recommendations and personal stories regarding their own experiences.

- Then, find out if your loved one's doctor provides care at any local nursing homes. If so, it might be possible to get him/her admitted there.

- Finally, if your loved one is in the hospital, ask the social worker about discharge planning. He/she should be able to help you find a nursing home that meets the family's needs.

The second step in the process is to compare the quality of the nursing homes you're considering. That may seem to be an overwhelming task. Lucky for us, the last several years have brought some easier ways to accomplish this:

- *www.medicare.gov/nursinghomecompare/search.html* compares the quality of every Medicare- and Medicaid-certified nursing home in the country to a universal set of standards. Input the name of each facility you are considering to see how it stacks up against the norm.

- Call the office of your county's long-term-care ombudsman, who serves as an advocate for nursing homes resident. These civil servants can provide a wealth of helpful information. Here, too, you can raise questions about the various facilities and get direct answers from someone whose business it is supposed to be to respond factually.

- Your state's Office of Health Care Quality (OHCQ) is responsible for licensing and certifying nursing home facilities and other agencies. It is charged with monitoring each facility's quality of care. OHCQ conducts unannounced surveys to determine compliance with rules and regulations. You can check survey results on their web page or look for them to be posted in the nursing home's lobby.

The third step is to actually visit the two or three nursing homes you have chosen using steps one and two above.

- Consider what's important to you and your loved one and visit with a list of questions to ask. Here are some ideas: Does the patient get to choose what time to get up, go to sleep, or bathe? Can the patient have visitors at any time? Can the patient's living space be decorated any way the patient desires? Are there set meal times?

- Nursing home residents have guaranteed rights and protections, such as being treated respectfully. When you visit, ask for a copy of the residents' Bill of Rights.

- Visit the nursing home once with an appointment so you can be shown around. Then, visit at different times of the day or on weekends without an appointment. Notice how the place functions without full staff and/or in the absence of management.

- If convenient, speak to a resident or a resident's family member about their experiences in the facility.

Finally, family members need to be ready to transition from care givers to care advocates. Without an effective advocate for the nursing home resident, the likelihood of problems caused by the lack of good care greatly increases. It's the old "squeaky wheel gets the grease" story. You must stay engaged to ensure your loved one gets the high-quality level of care you expect and he/she deserves.

The National Consumer Voice for Quality Long Term Care, *www.theconsumervoice.org*, has replaced the Citizens' Coalition for Nursing Home Reform (NCCNHR). Its website has more information on long-term care issues than you can absorb in one or two sittings. If you must put a family member in a nursing home or are considering it, I urge you to look at the materials from this group.

The Medicare/Medicaid publication, *A Consumer Guide to Choosing a Nursing Home*, is another valuable resource. The guide's purpose is to help prospective residents and their friends and family members navigate consumer information resources, understand the information and make an informed choice. It can be downloaded from the *www.medicare.gov* website or from the information clearinghouse at *www.theconsumervoice.org*. Also, you can get a free copy by calling 1-800-633-4227.

The magazine, *U.S. News & World Reports*, publishes annual lists of the "best" of things – colleges, towns, etc. You can read their report on the best nursing homes in each state by entering "Nursing Home Ratings" in "your state's name" in your computer browser. It also provides a report entitled "How to Choose a Nursing Home." A lot can be found out about how facilities are rated, but nothing is better than a personal, hands-on review and your own investigation.

There are many wonderful nursing homes and, unfortunately, many not so wonderful ones that are best avoided. If time allows, you should do a lot of research and make several personal visits to make an informed choice. Consider whether you would want to live in a particular place when you are older. Then, let your conscience, your pocketbook and your good judgment be your guide.

Preparing for the Cost

of

Long-term Care

by

Jacqueline D. Byrd and Patricia A. Davis

Imagine this: You are 45-years old and your spouse is 43. You have one child, age 12. You own your home that is worth approximately $200,000, carry a mortgage of $150,000, and have very little in savings. Both of you work and live a modest, but comfortable lifestyle. In addition, you have combined retirement accounts of $130,000 ($60,000 in the wife's 401(k) and $70,000 in the husband's IRA) and expect to work another 15 to 20 years.

However, something about your spouse's health doesn't seem exactly right and tragedy strikes. The diagnosis is Lou Gehrig's disease and your spouse is no longer able to work. The doctor tells you your spouse most likely will not be able to walk much longer and, within the next six months, will probably require in-home care. The doctor goes on to say that it is also very likely that your spouse will require nursing home care for a number of months (perhaps 38 to 60 months) before death caused by this horrible disease.

Let's say you have some disability insurance that supplies sufficient income for the two of you to take care of basic expenses. However, neither disability insurance, health insurance nor Medicare will provide sufficient coverage for extended nursing home care.

Based on counsel from the doctor, you expect that in approximately two years, your spouse will require long-term care with nursing home and prescription expenses of approximately $8,000 to $10,000 per month (maybe more two years from now). Perhaps, by then, your spouse will have become eligible for disability payments providing approximately $2,500 per month in income. Your own income is about $2,500 per month. As a last resort, you must consider Medicaid coverage.

Medicaid? Here is what that picture looks like to most people: you will first spend all of your money; then, your spouse can go on Medicaid. When your spouse dies, you will have next to nothing to live on and no retirement savings. This is a bleak picture indeed. Are there other options? Yes. The best option is to plan and plan early enough for your choices to have the desired results.

There is an insurance product designed to help pay for health care situations such as this one. It is called **long-term-care insurance (LTCI.)** Your LTCI policy takes effect once you satisfy its conditions, such as needing assistance with several daily living activities. Once this happens, you may begin claiming benefits from your insurance company and receiving a daily or monthly amount, depending on your policy's details. These benefits are then used to pay for the care you'll need.

You can continue to receive these benefits for as long as you need to or until your coverage period, usually 3-5 years, is up. LTCI policies have a variety of features. The "basket of features" includes:

- **Benefit Period:** This refers to the total amount of time the insurer will cover your claims and benefits. The period can be set for a certain number of years or you can choose to be covered for the rest of your life. (The benefit period is a major driver of your premium cost.)

- **Elimination Period**: The elimination period is commonly referred to as the **waiting period**. This is the amount of time you have to cover your own expenses before your policy starts paying claims. A longer elimination period can lessen the cost of your premiums. (Choices usually run from 1-6 months.)

- **Daily Benefit**: This refers to the maximum amount that your long-term-care policy will pay daily. The daily benefit is one of the main long-term-care options you need to decide about. The benefit amount you want is directly related to the care cost in the state/area where you live now or will when the care is provided.

- **Inflation Protection**: Inflation protection is a crucial element of a LTCI policy. With the rising cost of long-term care and the likelihood that you may need services way into the future, this ensures your benefits can keep up with inflationary rate increases.

- **Spousal Discount:** This feature reduces a policy's cost if partners or a married couple decide to buy LTCI from the same company.

In the case described in the opening paragraph, LTCI can be a very good solution but you and your spouse are in your 40s and most likely had never given long-term-care insurance any thought. Now, of course, your spouse will not pass the underwriting. However, buying such a policy is a solution you should seriously consider for yourself to protect your family and its assets from the costs of your own possible disability. Even if you can pass underwriting requirements yourself, you might not be able to afford the insurance since it is relatively expensive at your age. (LTCI policy premiums are more costly the older you are when you buy the policy.) To learn more, google "long-term-care insurance." The booklet, "Guide to Long-Term-Care Insurance" is available at *www.pueblo.gsa.gov.*

Another option is Medicaid planning. You should know that it's never too early or too late to think about planning for the costs of long-term care. Medicaid laws allow you to preserve some assets under various circumstances and rules. However, you shouldn't rely on the "word on the street," but should check with a professional as there are risks involved in Medicaid planning, including look-back periods, possible disqualifications and estate-recovery rules.

Most of us actually avoid even thinking about the issues of incapacity and death and, unfortunately, do not engage in the necessary planning about funding our own long-term care needs. In Maryland, for instance, the state where we live, retirement plans of the individual requiring care and his/her spouse are at risk. So are Section 529 plans he/she may have set up for his/her grandchildren. All are required to be liquidated and funds expended before Medicaid eligibility. This unfortunate situation causes many to even contemplate divorcing a much-loved spouse. (Please check with an elder law professional before taking such drastic action. There are other legal options available to you.)

Remember that the law specifically prohibits nursing homes from requiring a third-party guarantee of payment. You can sign to pay the bill from the resident's resources and you can voluntarily sign to assume personal responsibility for the bill. Just make sure you don't do any of it by accident. Read the contract carefully. It would be best to ask your elder law attorney to review the contract before the final signing. The cost of such a review will be much lower than the cost of making a mistake in this critical area.

Furthermore, there has been great progress in removal of the Medicare "Improvement Standard" for nursing homes. At one time, patients regularly were told, "Medicare won't pay any longer because you don't need skilled care." Under current law, nursing homes and Medicare are no longer allowed to use that standard. A nursing home patient must continue receiving rehab services to maintain the strength and abilities he/she possessed when admitted to the facility. Even so, it's important to remember Medicare only covers up to 100 days of nursing home care, per stay.

Life is full of unknown risks:

- How long will you live past retirement?

- How far will the money you have stretch?

- What happens if one spouse becomes incapacitated?

Until now, whatever you saved in your retirement plans (IRAs, 401(k)s, etc.) was yours to use in retirement and that was the one "known piece" of the puzzle. With rising health care costs, the slow pace of the economy, and the government's constant need to address shortfalls, the "known piece" is now also being threatened. There is a wealth of information on this topic at *www.longtermcarelink.net*. Click on "Books and Information." Additional resources are shown in Appendix D.

Even thinking about long-term care and its financial implications can be frightening. The intent here is to take some of the mystery out of it and direct you to known resources - websites, printed material and legal professionals - that will help you determine the best planning solution for you and your family. Hope this helps.

VII. COMMON MONEY SCAMS

(Protecting yourself and

your loved ones)

What Would Mimi Say

about

Money Scams?

❖ All that glitters is not gold.

❖ There is none so blind as he who will not see.

❖ Why does everything always have to be so hind-sighted?

❖ A fool and his money are soon parted.

❖ A bird in the hand is worth two in the bush.

❖ You can't get something for nothing.

❖ If it sounds too good to be true…You know the rest!

❖ I know I taught you better than that!

COMMON MONEY SCAMS

It is expected that, as members of the sandwich generation, you (and your parents) have at least begun to put aside money to use later. Unfortunately, there is a large cadre of unscrupulous individuals who is aware of that and stay up nights trying to invent new ways to swindle you out of your cash. These scams come in many different forms and keep government agencies like the FBI, Consumer Protection Bureau, Department of Justice and many others busy alerting consumers to the latest scams, teaching you how to protect yourself against them, and tracking down and prosecuting the offenders.

According to Citizens Advice, a non-profit that helps people resolve their legal, money and other problems by providing free independent advice and counseling, more than 22,000 people were scammed in 2012. The FBI cautions that the "over-40 crowd," especially seniors, is often targeted by con artists for the following reasons:

- This group is most likely to have a sizable "nest egg."

- They are likely to be homeowners.

- Many have excellent credit.

- Most are too polite to hang up on strangers or to close the door in their faces without listening to their spiel.

To keep you informed and keep your hard-earned money in your pocket to use when you are ready, following is a description of some of the "secret" scams and tactics used that you might not have heard of. These and many others are listed on various websites such as *www.usa.gov*, *www.cnn.money*, *www.scamguard.com*, *www.bankrate.com* and *www.aarp.com*.

- **Door-to-Door Scams**:

  ❖ **Home Maintenance Services** - You are given a cheap quote that requires an up-front deposit. The scammer either disappears with your money or raises the price and performs sub-par work.

  ❖ **Fake Energy-saving Gadget** - You are sold a device that, when plugged in, the seller claims, will lower your energy bill by as much as 40%. The device does nothing to lower your bill.

  ❖ **Fake Green Deal Sales** - You are told you are entitled to a large sum of money to fund Green Deal home improvements such as insulation or a new boiler. You are then asked to pay an administrative fee to cover processing and shipping. You never see the scammer again after you have paid your money.

- **"Too Good To Be True" Scams**:

  ❖ **Fake Dates** - You meet a person through a dating website and, before long, the person is asking you for money to cover real or imaginary bills. You send the requested money and, essentially, say goodbye to the potential suitor unless he/she calls again requesting more money.

  ❖ **Training Course Scam** - You are advised you are the selected applicant for a high-salaried job that you apply for online. You then are told you must enroll in and pay for a training course of some kind to ensure you're ready for the new position.

  ❖ **Tax Back** - You receive an e-mail from a fraudulent group claiming you are entitled to a tax refund but that first you must confirm your personal details. They then use this information either to drain your bank account or create an identity for themselves using your information.

❖ **Pension Problems** - You are contacted by a person, supposedly from The Pension Helpline, stating you are due a large bonus from the government due to underpayment of your pension. To get the bonus, you must first provide a host of identifying information, including your bank account number, plus other personal data - just what's needed for identity theft.

❖ **Noise Rebatement** - In this one, you are contacted by a supposed "government representative" advising you there may be monies owed to you because a former employer has been shut down because of noise. You are told you must pay a fee to get further information.

• **Scams Which Prey on Your Fears**:

❖ **Missed Payments** - You are called and told you are behind in your payments to a utility or credit card company and are asked to pay immediately over the phone - either via credit card or a direct debit to your checking account.

❖ **Medical Emergency** - You are called and told a loved one has been in an accident abroad. (You can hear him/her screaming in agony in the background.) The caller requests that you send money immediately to cover medical expenses.

❖ **Jury Duty Scam** - You are called and told you did not show up for jury duty. You reply that you never received a notice to come for jury duty. The caller then asks you to verify your personal information so he/she can be sure they have the "right person." They then tell you that a mistake has been made and apologize for the mix up. However, by then, you have given them all the data they need to create a false identity. No such notice was ever sent.

❖ **Tax Scam** - You are called and told you owe the IRS and that a payment must be made immediately over the phone. You bite. By the time the call is over, the caller has elicited enough personal data from you to create a fake ID.

❖ **Courier scams** - You are called on your landline supposedly by your bank and told that fraudsters have used your debit or credit card and it needs to be replaced. You call your bank on the number given to you by the fraudsters and the bank confirms this. You are told to key in your pin number and hand over your card to a courier who will arrive soon. However, between receiving the call and dialing "your bank" you didn't hear a dial tone and are actually still speaking to the scammers, who never disconnected the line.

● **Misleading (or Shady) Sales Tactics and Practices**:

❖ **Affinity Fraud** - Scammers often hire salespeople to target specific religious, ethnic, social or professional groups. Usually, the salesperson is a member of the same group as the target, thus increasing his/her credibility. Once trust is obtained and one person invests or makes a purchase, then the fraud is perpetrated on others in the same group who are then willing to consider becoming involved.

❖ **Churning** - This occurs when a securities professional makes unnecessary trades or exchanges to generate commissions. Churning happens most often when your broker has your permission to make trades in your account without prior authorization.

❖ **Guaranteed Returns** - You are promised a high return on a particular security product. Sandwich generation-ers may be especially interested in this as a way of quickly increasing the size of their retirement fund, which many know to be woefully inadequate. You should know it is illegal for legitimate brokers and financial advisers to guarantee a specific rate of return on a securities product.

❖ **Free Meal Seminars** - This one is especially popular with seniors. Potential investors are invited to a free investment seminar held at a popular (and sometimes expensive) local restaurant. Investment opportunities are presented to the group and follow-up appointments are made to conduct free one-on-one sessions with attendees often to convince them to replace their current investments with some that are either inappropriate or have high fees. In any event, these meal seminars are also a way of obtaining your personal information.

❖ **Mortgage Loan Fraud** - In this instance, scammers offer to refinance a homeowner's property at a very low interest rate. Often, the "lender" either is a fraud or does not actually own the property. Once the "closing" is held and the property is signed over to the new "lender," the promised money often doesn't come. For months or maybe even years, you believe your home has been refinanced until you receive an eviction notice and learn you no longer own your home. By then, it's usually too late to reverse the transaction.

- **Securities Fraud:**

  ❖ **Ponzi Schemes** - These were described earlier in Chapter III. Basically, such schemes consist of using the money obtained from new investors to pay early investors exorbitant returns. This scheme usually works as long as the scammers continue to generate enough dollars from new clients to pay the promised returns to the earlier ones. Once there are no more new clients, the scam falls apart and usually all the investors - new and old - lose the money they have invested.

  ❖ **"Pump and Dump" Scams** - Brokers and other unscrupulous individuals artificially inflate a stock's value. When other investors start buying the stock, then they sell or "dump" the stock, rendering the shares held by John Q. Public virtually worthless.

- **Unregistered Activities**:

  ❖ **Investment Products** - Scammers often try to sell unsuspecting consumers investment products that are not real or registered. Legitimate products are required by law to be registered. Before buying, check with your local or federal regulators to confirm the product's legitimacy.

  ❖ **Brokers and Financial Advisors** - Both are required by law to be registered with federal regulators. Before entrusting your funds to either, confirm their legitimacy. This can be done at *www.licensedbroker.gov.*

- **Car-buying Scams:**

  ❖ **Internet Purchase Scam** - Recently, the federal government has received a significant number of complaints from consumers who have "purchased" cars over the internet for which they have paid but have yet to receive their merchandise. Payment is usually made via Western Union or wire transfer. At that point, the money is gone and the car is never received.

  ❖ **Used Car Scam** - As money becomes tighter, more and more families are buying used cars than ever before. Unfortunately, some law enforcement agencies are reporting that VIN cloning - which targets used car buyers - is on the rise and the Better Business Bureau (BBB) advises car buyers to do their research or they could unknowingly buy a stolen car.

- **Misuse of Better Business Bureau Trademark Scam -** The BBB has issued an international alert to warn about people misusing the BBB and BBBOnLine trademarks to extort money from online car shoppers. The BBB received an inquiry from an online shopper who was searching for an automobile on *www.cars.com.* The shopper was sent an invoice by e-mail from someone posing as an escrow service that displayed a cars.com and BBBOnLine banner and listed several other BBB sites. The fraudulent e-mail invoice contained claims that the BBB and cars.com are trusted, neutral third parties. There was no affiliation.

- **Phony Escrow Company Scam** - To combat the spread of this scam, the BBB has issued an alert to warn online car shoppers that scammers are posing as phony escrow services to defraud consumers out of thousands of dollars. Internet thieves are now using escrow service fronts with some new twists to steal money and personal identities. They supposedly "hold" the purchaser's money until the deal has been concluded.

Credit Card Protection Act - The 2009 Credit Card Accountability Responsibility & Disclosure (CARD) Act brought about sweeping protections for consumers in the areas of fees, payments and interest rates. Below are some of the Act's provisions that credit card companies must adhere to in the three areas mentioned.

- Fees:

  - Cannot charge a late payment fee that is greater than your minimum payment.

  - Cannot charge you an inactivity fee for not using your card.

  - Cannot charge you more than one fee for a single late payment or any other violation of your cardholder agreement.

  - Cannot charge you over-the-limit transaction fees unless you opt in, stating you agree to allow transactions that take you over your credit card limit. If the credit card company allows the transaction without your opt-in, it cannot charge you a fee.

  - Can only impose one fee per billing cycle for transactions that take you over your credit limit if you opt in to over-the-limit transactions. You can revoke your opt-in at any time.

- Payments:

  ❖ Must tell you how long it will take to pay off your balance if you make only minimum payments.

  ❖ Must mail or deliver your credit card bill at least 21 days before your payment is due.

  ❖ Must apply any payments above the minimum required amount to the balance with the highest interest rate, if you have more than one rate.

- Interest Rates:

  ❖ Cannot increase your rate for the first 12 months after you open an account, unless you have a variable interest rate or an introductory rate; you are more than 60 days late paying your bill; or you are in a workout agreement and don't make payments as arranged.

  ❖ Cannot charge higher rates for purchases made before you receive notice of a new rate.

  ❖ Cannot use the double-cycle billing method when calculating interest; interest can only be charged on balances within the current billing cycle. (Double-cycle billing takes into account the average daily balance of both the current billing cycle and the previous cycle. It can add a significant amount of interest charges to customers whose average balance varies greatly from month to month.)

  ❖ Cannot increase your Annual Percentage Rate (APR) without explaining why. If your credit card company increases your APR, it generally must re-evaluate that new rate increase every six months. Under some circumstances, it may have to reduce your rate after the evaluation.

❖ Can issue credit cards to consumers under age 21 only if the cardholder can show they are able to make payments or have a parental or guardian co-signer.

As mentioned, the websites listed earlier have information on hundreds of scams. Financial scams described on these sites include those related to areas such as ATMs, banking, check fraud, travel, education, telephone, identity theft, Nigerian Letter fraud, reverse mortgages, home repair, work-at-home, and prize winnings, to name a few. The information presented is extremely educational and goes a long way toward helping you protect yourself and your loved ones.

Remember Mimi's warnings that "All that glitters is not gold;" and that "If it looks too good to be true…you know the rest!"

VIII. Secret Ways

to

IMPROVE YOUR FINANCES

(Making your money last longer and go further)

What Would Mimi Say

about

Improving Your Finances?

❖ You look out for the nickels and dimes and the dollars will take care of themselves.

❖ Pennies make dollars.

❖ You can't spend it but once.

❖ Save some for a rainy day.

❖ Money spent is money gone.

❖ Every penny counts.

Tips

to

Improve Your Finances

Caught between two generations that need assistance, many baby boomers, GenXers, and other members of the sandwich generation are feeling their time and resources ebbing away, leaving them ill-at-ease today and anxious about their future. Some may be tempted to tap their retirement accounts to help themselves or a loved one, which only adds to their financial burden.

When I think about the way Mimi and others in her generation managed to do so much with so little, it is unfathomable to me that, in this day and time, when many of us have resources her generation could never have dreamed of, we still struggle to make it. Perhaps their limited resources forced them to be so smart, out of necessity. But, smart they were.

There are books, courses, videos, websites - you name it, related to helping us make informed money-management decisions. Applying some basic common sense rules will help many stay on course and others get back on course and improve their finances. Experience and education tell me that the following rules work:

1. **Live below (not within) your means**. If you don't, your upkeep will be your downfall.

2. **Never underestimate the power of not spending**. You might be surprised at how much you could end up saving and have available when you really need it.

3. **Before you buy something, define the need; determine the cost; and list the alternatives**. Then ask yourself, "Is this a need or a want? Can I afford it? Should I afford it?"

4. **Beware of little expenses.** As Benjamin Franklin said, " ... Even a small leak can sink a big ship." Mimi reminded us constantly that "Pennies make dollars;" and "You look out for the nickels and dimes and the dollars will take care of themselves."

> *At one time, the county I live in contracted with me to do a series of money management classes for unemployed constituents. The thought was, when they got jobs, they would know how to handle their money. One day, after looking around the classroom, I made a comment that one of the biggest problems many of them had was on the other side of the wall from our classroom - the canteen. Several of them had bought bottled water at $1.25 per bottle, despite the fact they had no jobs and claimed to have no money. When I commented that they could get 24 bottles of water on sale at Target for $3.99 and bring water from home, one student exclaimed that she wanted her water cold! I responded that she could put her water in the freezer and bring it to class with her. Even the canteen water eventually gets warm. She hadn't thought of that.*

> *In yet another example in that same series, at the break, I saw one of the students outside smoking. She had claimed she had no money to save. When I pointed out that the cigarette money is money she could be saving, her response was, "Oh, I get these cheap. I go up to Delaware and get them. They don't have state tax!"*

Never mind the gas and tolls it takes to get from Maryland to Delaware and back.

5. **Have only one or two credit cards and use them for convenience, not for credit, except in emergencies.** You must have at least one active credit card to have a credit score. A credit card may make you eligible for discounts, may be required to rent a car or confirm a hotel room, and may be necessary for you to be able to turn on utilities in your name. Also, in the event of a dispute, not only have you not put up cash, but also you have the power of a major credit card company to help you settle with the vendor.

    Remember, 1) you should only buy items on credit that you would and could have purchased with cash; and 2) you should pay for the items as quickly as you can, to minimize interest charges.

To help readers learn how to do a better job with their finances, many financial publications, writers and bloggers are weighing in on this topic. Publications such as *US News Money, Frugal Living,* the *AARP Magazine, PTMoney* and many others have written extensively on the subject. Their working theory is that, despite the recent uptick in the economy and improvement in the unemployment statistics, consumers still relish money-saving ideas and tips on ways to improve their financial situation.

Many of the suggested actions are very familiar, while others are not as well known. The objective is to provide you with useful information to help improve your finances and to make a better life for you and your family. Below is a list of 25 recommendations you might find helpful to improve your own finances or those of a loved one.

1. **Set goals.** You can't spend your money on the things that are important to you if you don't know what those things are. (There's an old saying: "If you don't know where you're going, any road will take you there.") Write down your major financial goals and the timing associated with each. For example, reduce outstanding MasterCard bill by 50% by June 1; refinance the house by September 15; pay off all payday loans by December 31. The goals must be **SMART**, i.e., **S**pecific, **M**easurable, **A**ttainable, **R**ealistic, and **T**ime-bound.

   Once you've set your goals, you can determine whether your income and expense patterns are consistent with the goals you have for yourself and your family. If they're not and a goal is really important, then, identify and make the changes needed for you to achieve your goal.

2. **Share your goals with family and friends.** Talking about your goals to others usually will help you continue to focus on them. A lecturer once told audience members to share "give up goals" but not "going up goals." The speaker indicated folks will remind you that you said you were going to give something up ("give up goal") if they see you violating your own rule. On the other hand, many times, people try to discourage you from doing things to improve your own situation ("going up goals"), especially if doing so puts you ahead of where they are or where they want to be.

3. **Work a little each day on your major goals**. The "baby steps" you make each day soon will add up to "big steps." Eventually, you will meet your goal. Be patient with yourself and never give up, if the goal is important. If it isn't, then it shouldn't have been on the list to begin with.

4. **Create a 12-month spending plan.** This comprehensive plan (or budget) should list all of your expected income and expenditures for a full year. A longer-range plan enables you to look at your income and expenses over an extended period of time and makes it easier for you to notice any categories that may have been missed such as tax refunds, holiday bonuses, birthdays (family and friends), auto registration and driver's license renewals.

5. **Pay off (or pay down) as much debt as possible**. Nothing will drag you down faster than a mountain of debt. Make this the year you finally get all of your credit cards and loans paid off or at least significantly reduced, especially the high-cost debt. This is particularly true of student loans which, by the way, are **not** dischargeable via bankruptcy.

6. **Build up your savings**. Having a substantial savings account is necessary in the event there are unanticipated expenses. Not only does having a ready source of cash give you peace of mind, but also it provides you with a nest egg to handle unbudgeted, sudden, or higher-than-planned cash needs.

7. **Work toward cutting your expenses in virtually every major expense category**. This often requires

cooperation from family members, but take the first step and vow to bring the others along with you. A major reduction in areas like utility bills, gas bills, food bills and interest charges will significantly reduce your expenses. Toward that same end, keep a spending diary to record all of your expenditures for a month. (The results may surprise you.) Going back and reviewing the diary makes you aware of where your money goes and where you might be able to cut back.

8. **Identify new income streams.** Having more than one source of income provides an alternative if your primary source of income gets interrupted. It also makes the loss of that major income stream less devastating. There are people willing to pay for talents you have that you may have looked at only as hobbies. For example, cooking, sewing, painting, photography and event planning are skills many don't have and are willing to pay for.

9. **Negotiate for purchases.** This is especially beneficial for big-ticket items such as cars, furniture, electronics and real estate. In an economy where many retailers' sales are down, most would rather sell at a lower price than hold onto the merchandise while they wait for a full-price buyer. Your aggressiveness and their willingness to compromise can result in tremendous savings for you, the customer. Don't hesitate to try it.

10. **Eliminate spending temptations** by unsubscribing to store e-mail alerts, catalogs, credit card offers and other retail notifications. They only tempt you to spend money you may not have on items you probably don't need.

11. **Protect your privacy!** Closely guard things like your passwords and PINs; Social Security, bank account, credit card, and health insurance/Medicare numbers; and any other personal information an identity thief could use. When asked for this information, be sure you understand why it is needed, how it will be used, and how it will be protected. This is true of e-mail, telephone or in-person requests. Also, buy and use a cross-cut shredder to destroy documents with personal information. Never give this information to a telemarketer or to any stranger.

12. **Learn to prepare home-cooked meals**. Eating out regularly can be an enormous expense. By the same token, cooking and eating at home can be healthier, cheaper and even tastier. If you aren't an accomplished chef, The Food Network channel and the internet both have a ton of free information to help you quickly learn the ropes.

That same client who I mentioned earlier with the $3,600 shortfall had a 9 year-old son, Rodney, whose Grandfather picked him up from school every day. Rodney didn't like any of the food Grandpa had at his house, so the two of them went to a fast food restaurant after Grandpa picked Rodney up.

Not only was eating fast food each day unhealthy, but also it was expensive. Some days Grandpa was hungry too. More money.

I suggested that she figure out what Rodney did like to eat, purchase it at the grocery store, and take the food to Grandpa's house each Sunday night. That way, it would be there for Rodney each day when he came home from school.

She took my suggestion and ended up with cash she could use to close that $3.600 gap.

13. **Calculate your retirement income needs.** Run the numbers and be sure your current savings level will support your desired retirement lifestyle. If it doesn't, then ramp up your retirement savings to such a level that will ensure you can afford to live the way you want in retirement. If that is not possible, then either reduce current expenses or agree to live a more modest retirement lifestyle. (See Appendix C for an example of retirement funding and Appendix D for online retirement funding calculation sites.)

14. **Send for copies of your three credit reports at least annually and work to improve your credit score, if needed**. By law, each consumer is entitled to one free credit report annually from each of the three major credit bureaus - Experian, TransUnion and Equifax. (You can get a free copy of your consolidated report from the website *www.annualcreditreport.com*.) The reports are free, but you may have to pay for your actual credit score. Be sure to check for and immediately correct any errors you find in your credit reports. (See Appendix D for contact information for each credit bureau.)

15. **Protect your credit score**. To remain in good standing with your creditors, always make at least the minimum

credit card payment required and ensure all payments are made on time.

16. **Take full advantage of benefits offered by your employer**. This includes things like gym memberships; financial planning and tax preparation assistance; insurance coverage for you and your dependents; flexible spending accounts (both medical and childcare); discounted employee stock purchase plans; and any 401(k) match. Most of these are non-taxable to the employee and save you the out-of-pocket expense of having to pay for these services yourself with after-tax dollars.

17. **Look for less expensive and more creative ways to give**. Try to find out a gift recipient's likes, needs and wants and give a gift that reflects those desires. People often appreciate something handmade, home-baked, painted, or built by the gift giver, or a meaningful experience. Such a gift will probably end up being a lot less expensive than a "thing" you would buy. In addition, the family member or friend is likely to be touched by your thoughtfulness and impressed with your creativity.

18. **Be sure your estate planning documents are in order**. We all have read the stories about situations where a decedent's estate is left in shambles, creating a mess for the heirs to untangle. These documents become your voice when you cannot speak for yourself. In particular, if you have a minor child, at a minimum, name a guardian for that child. Otherwise, your state will do it for you.

19. **Find your perfect piece of plastic.** If your credit card isn't meeting all your needs, then it is time to find a card that does. Comparison websites such as *www.nerdwallet.com, www.creditcards.com* and *www.indexcreditcards.com* make it easy to compare the benefits of different cards to figure out which one suits your needs. If you carry any balance, focus on finding the card with the lowest interest rate. You can choose from cards that give you points, cash back, miles or other consumer products. Opt for the one that suits you best.

20. **Invest in college savings plans for yourself or minor children who you want to help.** There are various college payment plans available from Section 529 and Coverdell college savings plans that allow you to invest after-tax money that then grows federal tax-free, to prepaid tuition plans that lock in prices at the time of the contract. (With the Coverdell account, the term "qualified expenses" also includes primary and secondary schools, not just colleges and universities. Though similar to a Section 529 Plan, there are differences. So, be sure to check them out before signing up.) If you invest in a state-supported Section 529 plan, you may be eligible for a state tax deduction in addition to the federal tax deduction. These plans can be used for you, as well as for a loved one. Also, several insurance companies advertise college savings plans, combined with a non-cancellable insurance component, that are worth looking at.

21. **Educate your children about finances.** This is a skill set that will last them a lifetime. They are never too young for you to start the learning process.

> *Mimi made us learn the rules of the money game at an early age, and we are now very grateful she did. At the time, however, we thought she was just being mean and stingy. She gave each of the five of us an allowance every other Monday – the same day she got paid from her federal government job. We were not allowed to come into her bedroom, where she had the cash laid out in piles to cover her obligations, until she told us to enter. When we were given the green light, we were then handed our money with the clear understanding that 1) we could do whatever we wanted with it whenever we wanted; and 2) there would be no more until two weeks from then. If you ran out before then, too bad.*

> *No, we did not know the word "budget," but, we did know we'd better make our allowance last for two weeks. I remember saying to her one day, "Mischelle's Mother gives her money whenever she asks for it." Her response was, "Do I look like Mischelle's Mother?" She always knew she was right and was never swayed by our pleas. It wasn't until much, much later we came to realize 1) she didn't have it to give us; and 2) she was trying to stretch what she did have. The lights stayed on; the water ran; we were never hungry; and there were never any bill collectors calling.*

There aren't many Mimi's around, but there are many free, web-based programs and sites available to help you learn the ropes.

Websites for some of the more popular free ones that are loaded with information, games, books, videos, etc., include: *www.jumpstart.org; www.mymoney.gov; www.moneysmart.org; www.SchwabMoneyWise.com; www.moneysmart.org;* and *ww.Creativewealthintl.org.*

(The latter is the website for the fun-filled Camp Millionaire financial literacy program for kids, teens and adults that I am a licensed to teach. For more information, go to its site or to my website at *www.yourmoneywiz.com.*) As you practice the skills taught in these valuable programs, you can reinforce the messages with your children by your own smart money choices. Pay it forward.

22. **Annually review your Social Security Administration Benefits Statement**. Look at the statement to ensure you have received proper credit for all the years you've worked and paid into the Social Security Trust Fund. This annual statement provides the basis for the amount of your Social Security retirement benefit. Any incorrect entry on your statement could mean an error in the calculation of your monthly benefit. Your review will give you a sense of whether there are any additional funds that need to be generated for retirement to allow you to live your desired lifestyle.

23. **Familiarize yourself with discount/coupon websites such as** *www.groupon.com, www.retailmenot.com,*

www.opentable.com, www.couponcabin.com, www.e-bates.com and www.slickdeals.com.

Such sites offer a variety of coupons at retailers and restaurants widely used by the average consumer. Also, the AARP website, *www.aarp.com*, has information about a multitude of discounts available to seniors.

24.   **Consider a yard sale to get rid of un-needed stuff and generate extra cash**. The saying, "One man's junk is another man's treasure" couldn't be truer. Instead of just keeping unwanted items piled up in the back of the closet or in a box in the basement, join forces with friends and neighbors and have a yard sale to generate extra funds, to clean out and better organize your living space, and to offer items to others who may be able to use them.

25.   **Work with a retirement planner or financial advisor to regularly rebalance your portfolio and ensure you are still on track to meet your retirement goals.**

Remember, you are the greatest asset you have on your journey to achieving the lifestyle you want. Think about the future you'd like to have for yourself and your family and put into action a plan that will allow you to live that life. Not only will doing so help you think more positively about the future, but also it will help you make better choices today.

In the words of the well-know feminist, Gloria Steinem, "Rich people plan for four generations. Poor people plan for Saturday night." Let's compromise and plan for a couple of generations ahead. Your heirs be glad you did.

Appendix A

Creating a Spending Plan

A spending plan or budget is simply your GPS (Global Positioning System) to guide your income and expense patterns. It lists *ALL* of your expected income and expenses over the time period covered, which should be at least 6-12 months.

Preparing a budget takes work. But, in the end, it is well worth the effort because, if done properly, once the numbers are run and it is brought into balance, it allows you to freely operate within the limits set out in the plan. Also, if it is done accurately, it will help you determine whether you can afford the lifestyle you want to live.

To make this process work, do the following:

1. Gather all of the documentation you have that show your income and expenses over the last six months. To do this, you will need items such as:

    a) Check registers

    b) Bank statements

    c) Credit card statements

    d) Receipts/bills for expenses such as utilities, childcare, repairs, insurance and medical expenses

    e) Car payment coupon book

    f) Mortgage/ rent payment book

    g) Pay stubs

    h) Tax returns

    i) Other, such as tip records, gifts, etc.

2. Make a separate pile containing the receipts/documentation for each expense category. This includes items such as:

   a) Housing - including rent or mortgage payments, taxes, insurance , HOA fees, and maintenance/repairs

   b) Transportation - including car payment, repairs and maintenance, gasoline, tags, insurance, road service, parking, and vehicle personal property taxes, if applicable

   c) Food

   d) Utilities - including electricity, gas, water, alarm monitoring, phones (cell and land lines), cable, trash and water

   e) Personal – including clothing, hair, nails, laundry

   f) Savings - regular, retirement, and emergency

   g) Contributions and tithes

   h) Medical - including co-pays and prescriptions

   i) Insurance statements - including disability, life, and long-term-care

   j) Personal items - including hair and nails

   k) Gifts - including Christmas, birthdays, anniversary, etc.

   l) Outstanding debts - including student loans, existing credit cards

   m) Estimated federal and state taxes (if needed)

   n) Allowance

   o) Miscellaneous

3. Add up the receipts for each expense category and divide by the number of months of receipts you have. (This gives you your average monthly expense, by type and is a good number to start with.)

4. Make a listing of all of your income sources, by month, including beginning checking account balance, net salaries, pension income, Social Security benefits, tax refunds, child support, alimony, gifts, and any other income.

5. In a table, similar to the sample shown following these instructions, list all of the income and expenses from the steps above, in the appropriate months. When you finish, you should have accounted for essentially every dime of income and expenses you expect to receive or pay out. (A blank worksheet can be downloaded from my website: *www.yourmoneywiz.com.*

6. Total all of your income, by month; then do the same for all of your expenses, by month.

7. Subtract expenses from income, by month. (Some months will be positive; others may be negative.)

8. Add together all the monthly positives and negatives. If this total is negative, either find other sources of income or reduce expenses to make sure the total of the positives and negatives is zero or more. This will ensure your budget reflects a lifestyle you can afford.

This may be your first attempt at creating a detailed budget. Do not be concerned if you find that elements of it need to be changed. A budget is not fixed forever. Continue to tweak it until you feel it accurately reflects the life you want to live. Review it at least monthly, and make adjustments to it as warranted by any change in your life circumstances.

Changes to the budget may be needed when there is a new event, such as:

1. Salary adjustment

2. New job

3. New tax schedules

4. New family goals

5. A change in family status - marriage, divorce, separation

6. New family members

7. Significantly increased financial responsibilities, such as helping to support a family member in need

Treat your budget as a guide and not as a pair of handcuffs. Indeed, you can still do many of the things you want to do. The budget merely helps you determine the timing of doing them and points out choices you may have to make along the way. It should be done in such a way that it accurately and completely reflects you and your family's goals and the income needed to support those goals. Once you are certain of that, your budget can be a major tool to help you live within your means and to help light your path to financial freedom.

Budget Spreadsheet
For Sandwich Generation Couple
Page 1

RESOURCES & EXPENSES \ MONTH	JUL	AUG	SEP	OCT	NOV	DEC	TOTALS
CASH ON HAND	65						65
CHECKING ACCT BAL	375						375
CHECKS FOR DEPOSIT							0
CHG ACCT CREDITS							0
MONIES OWED TO YOU	25						25
SALARY (IES)							
YOU	2,500	2,500	2,500	2,500	2,500	2,500	15,000
YOUR SPOUSE	1,850	1,850	1,850	1,850	1,850	1,850	11,100
TAX REFUND				300			300
GIFTS	25	25	25	25	25	500	625
INTEREST / DIVIDENDS	12						12
OTHER							0
TOTAL RESOURCES	4,852	4,375	4,375	4,675	4,375	4,850	**27,502**

Budget Spreadsheet
For Sandwich Generation Couple
Page 2

RESOURCES & EXPENSES \ MONTH	JUL	AUG	SEP	OCT	NOV	DEC	TOTALS
WITHHOLDINGS--YOU:							
TAXES/ BENEFITS	800	800	800	800	800	800	4,800
401(K) PLAN	75	75	75	75	75	75	450
OTHER	12	12	12	12	12	12	72
WITHHOLDINGS--SPOUSE:							
TAXES/ BENEFITS	662	662	662	662	662	662	3,972
401(K) PLAN							0
OTHER	6	6	6	6	6	6	36
DONATIONS	20	20	20	30	20	30	140
SAVINGS	200	200	200	200	200	200	1,200
HOUSING:							
1ST MORTGAGE	917	917	917	917	917	917	5,502
2ND MORTGAGE							0
TAXES & INSURANCE	175	175	175	175	175	175	1,050
MAINTENANCE	50	50	50	50	50	50	300
LAWN CARE							0
FURNISHINGS / APPLIANCES					250		250
UTILITIES:							
GAS							0
ELECTRICITY	65	65	65	80	100	125	500
WATER	53		55		45		153
BURGLAR ALARM							0
CABLE	30	30	30	30	30	30	180
PHONE SERVICES:							
HOUSE PHONE	20	20	20	20	20	20	120
MOBILE PHONES	40	40	40	40	40	40	240
INTERNET ACCESS							0
NEWSPAPER							0
INSURANCE:							
AUTO	100	100	100	100	100	100	600
MEDICAL PRESCRIPTIONS/CO-PAYS	25	25	25	25	25	25	150
LIFE							0
LONG-TERM-CARE							0

Budget Spreadsheet
For Sandwich Generation Couple
Page 3

RESOURCES & EXPENSES \ MONTH	JUL	AUG	SEP	OCT	NOV	DEC	TOTALS
AUTO- RELATED EXP:							
CAR PAYMENT	155	155	155	155	155	155	930
TAGS / LICENSE			90				90
ROAD SERVICE					47		47
REPAIRS		100			200		300
GASOLINE	120	120	120	120	120	120	720
PARKING							0
CONSUMER LOANS:							
CREDIT UNION	60	60	60	60	60	60	360
VISA	125	125	125	125	125	125	750
EDUCATIONAL							0
CHILD/ELDER CARE	200	200	200	200	200	200	1,200
FOOD	225	225	225	225	225	225	1,350
CLOTHING	25	25	25	25	25	25	150
LAUNDRY/SHOE REPAIR	15	15	15	15	15	15	90
HAIR / HAIR PRODUCTS	25	25	80	25	25	80	260
TUITION							0
TRANSPORTATION	10	10	10	10	10	10	60
ENTERTAINMENT	25	50	25	25	50	25	200
VACATION (S)							0
GIFTS:							
BIRTHDAYS		50			50		100
CHRISTMAS						500	500
OTHER							0
ALLOWANCE:							
YOU	40	40	40	40	40	40	240
YOUR SPOUSE	40	40	40	40	40	40	240
MANICURIST							0
OTHER	50	50	50	50	50	50	300
	--------	--------	--------	--------	--------	--------	-----------
	-	-	-	-	-	-	-
TOTAL EXPENSES	4,313	4,437	4,512	4,337	4,964	4,937	27,502
	--------	--------	--------	--------	--------	--------	-----------
	-	-	-	-	-	-	-
MONTHLY PLUS/MINUS	537	-62	-137	338	-589	-87	**0**
CUMULATIVE BAL	537	475	338	676	87	**0**	

Appendix B

Calculating Your Retirement Income Needs

We all know how important it is to plan for the day when we no longer will generate income from a regular job. In other words, we need to plan for our retirement. Many people ask, "Where do I begin? How do I do it?" This appendix was written to help you answer those questions. Below are the steps you need to take, followed by an example.

(Chapter V is dedicated entirely to retirement planning. Appendix D, Resources, lists several automated on-line calculators that will "do the heavy lifting" (the actual calculations) for you.)

To calculate your retirement income needs:

1. **Start with your current annual income.** Then, estimate what percent of that amount you will need in retirement. Financial advisors usually recommend to clients that this percentage be 70%-100%, depending upon the retirement lifestyle you want.

2. **Estimate your total annual retirement income.** Your retirement income may come from one or more sources, such as:
   - Traditional pension
   - Social Security
   - IRA, 401(k), annuities
   - Other retirement plans
   - Investments

3. **Estimate your annual retirement expenses.** There are certain expenses you will no longer have such as a mortgage (if it has been paid off), commute costs, and daily lunches out. On the other hand, other expenses may be a bit higher like travel, utilities (if you expect to be home more), medical costs, and maintenance expenses for an aging house. These expenses **must** total less than your projected

retirement income or you will soon run out of money. Some common expenses include:

- Food and clothing
- Taxes – federal, state, local, personal property
- Housing
- Utilities
- Transportation – car payment, maintenance, gas, insurance, public transportation
- Health-care costs – Medicare, medicines, co-pays, deductibles
- Debts – consumer loans, student loans
- Travel
- Donations
- Gifts
- Education (for self or others)
- Personal care
- Care for others
- Savings

4. **Determine whether retirement income exceeds expenses.**

5. **If expenses exceed income, immediately start building a retirement fund to fill the gap.**

6. **Determine the age at which you wish to retire.**

7. **Estimate the annual rate of return you expect from your investments as well as the inflation rate to be used in your analysis.**

8. **Estimate your life span**, i.e., the number of years you expect to live in retirement.

The example on the next page uses the following assumptions:

1. You expect your retirement expenses to be $40,000 per year in today's dollars. This represents 80% of your current $50,000 annual income.
2. You are now 45 years old and expect to work another 22 years.
3. You expect to receive $36,000 per year in pension and Social Security income, at retirement.
4. You have already saved $75,000 toward your retirement, in addition to your 401(k) and IRA retirement savings.
5. Your 401(k) and IRA are valued at $50,000 today.
6. Your anticipated return on investments is 5%.
7. You expect an annual inflation rate of 2.5% per year.
8. You expect to live 18 years in retirement to the age of 85.

The calculation results on the next page show you do indeed have a funding gap. To close that gap, you need to save:

- $2,393 annually or
- $ 199 monthly or
- $ 63 bi-weekly.

Remember, your lifestyle in retirement is entirely up to you. If the amount you need to save to afford the lifestyle you want is too high, then look at alternatives. One would be to delay retirement; another would be to reduce your retirement expenses and be satisfied with a more modest lifestyle in retirement than the one you originally planned; a third would be to continue to work, while in retirement, at least part-time, to supplement your income. The key is to commit to begin and to stick to your plan so that you can live the life in retirement you want.

Sample Computation of Retirement Income Funding Needs

1. Amount required to duplicate purchasing power of $40,000 at 2.5% inflation 22 years from now (when you retire). $68,862

2. Minus projected annual Social Security/pension payments -$36,000

3. Remaining annual income target to be funded $32,862

4. Capital required to produce $32,862 annually at 5% for 18 years while in rerirement $384,143

5. Minus value of current capital assets of $75,000 at 5% for 22 years (until retirement) -$219,395

6. Minus combined value of retirement funds equal to $50,000 at 5% (includes 401(k) and IRA) for 22 years (until retirement) -$146,263

7. Additional capital required by retirement in 22 years $18,485

8. Annual savings required to be put aside at 5% per year for 22 years (until retirement) $2,393

9. Monthly savings required to be put aside at 5% per year for 22 years (until retirement) $199

10. Bi-weekly savings required to be put aside at 5% per year for 22 years (until retirement) $63

Note: For automated retirement income planning calculation tools, google "retirement income calculations" and input your specific parameters.

20 Money Management Mistakes to Avoid

Patricia Davis; B.S., M.B.A., M.S.

1. Not understanding your own/partner's financial views and values
2. Not having written, value-based financial goals
3. Choosing to be financially illiterate
4. Not making and adhering to a detailed budget
5. Not creating an emergency fund of at least 6 months of expenses
6. Perpetrating! Being a financial fraud!
7. Not seeking and paying for financial advice from trained pros
8. Not having your name on the title to property you "buy" with someone else
9. Co-signing your good credit away
10. Thinking your Will determines how your real estate assets get distributed upon your death, even those you hold in joint tenancy
11. Contracting for high-cost payday and title loans
12. Not annually checking your three free credit reports
13. Trusting anyone to "fix" your credit for a fee
14. Paying off debt with retirement savings or by refinancing your mortgage
15. Trusting your credit card and bank statements
16. Not saving for retirement by opening an IRA or contributing to your organization's retirement plan, especially if there is a match
17. Not fully understanding the concept of identity theft - what it is, what to look for, and how to protect yourself against it
18. Giving away your power when buying or leasing a car; focusing on the monthly payment rather than the deal itself, first
19. Not asking for discounts, especially if you are over 50
20. Believing federal student loans can be eliminated by filing for bankruptcy

Appendix D

Additional Helpful Resources

❖ Credit Reporting Agencies:

a) **Equifax**:
P.O. Box 740241
Atlanta, GA 30374
1-800-685-1111
www.equifax.com

b) **Experian**:
P.O. Box 20002
Allen, TX 75031
1-888-567-8688
www.experian.com

c) **TransUnion**:
P.O. Box 390
Chester, PA 19022
1-800-916-8880
www.transunion.com

d) **To get all three reports combined**:
www.annualcreditreport.com

❖ For Seniors:

a) **The National Council on the Aging;** *www.ncoa.org*
Works with partners to give older adults tools and information to stay healthy and secure.

b) **National Adult Day Services Association**
722 Grant Street, Suite L, Herndon, VA 20170
1-800-558-5301;
www.nadsa.org
Can refer you to adult day services in your parents' area.

c) **Life Answer booklets and Grandparent Information Center** - AARP
Grandparent Information Center
602 E St NW, Washington, DC 20049
Offers advice and information for grandparents.

d) **We Need to Talk...Family Conversations with Older Drivers** - The Hartford; 200 Executive Blvd, Southington, CT 06489;
www.thehartford.com/ talkwitholderdrivers

Contains materials for talking with older drivers and deciding when it is no longer safe for them to drive.

e) **Alzheimer's Association** - 225 N. Michigan Ave., Suite 1700, Chicago, IL 60601; 1-800-272-3900; *www.alz.org*
Provides information for families dealing with all forms of dementia

f) **Alzheimer's Disease Education and Referral Center**
P.O. Box 8250, Silver Spring, MD 20907; 1-800-438-4380
Has information on all aspects of Alzheimer's disease

g) **Children of Aging Parents**
1609 Woodbourne Road, Suite 302A, Levittown, PA 19057; 1-800-227-7294
www.caps4caregivers.org
Provides information on caregiving and referrals to support groups.

h) **Eldercare Locator** - 1-800-677-1116;
www.eldercare.gov
Provides information on aging services in your parents' area.

i) **National Association of Professional Geriatric Care Managers** - 1604 N. Country Rd, Tucson, AZ 85716
1-520-881-8008;
www.caremanager.org
Provides referrals to geriatric managers.

j) **National Family Caregivers Association**
10400 Connecticut Ave, Suite 500, Kensington, MD 20895
1-800-896-3650;
www.nfcacares.org
Offers newsletters and pamphlets on caregiving.

k) **Benefits Checkup** - *www.benefitscheckup.org*
Screens for public and private benefits and entitlement programs for people 55 and older.

l) **Centers for Medicare and Medicaid Services**
7500 Security Blvd, Baltimore, MD 21244;
1-877-267-2323;
www.cms.hhs.gov
Provides current information on both Medicare and Medicaid.

m) **Financial Planning Association**
1615 L. St. NW, Suite 650, Wash. DC 20036
1-800-282-7526;
www.fpanet.org
Offers information on selecting a financial planner, retirement planning, and financial security in old age. Also, gives referrals.

n) **GovBenefits -**
www.govbenefits.gov
Provides online screening to help determine eligibility for government benefits. Also provides agency contact information.

o) **Medicare Hotline -** 1-800-633-4277;
www.mwdicare.gov
Provides information on Medicare, Medicaid, Medigap and nursing homes. Also, reports on Medicare fraud and other illegal practices.

p) **Administration on Aging -**
www.aoa.gov/eldfam/eldfam.asp
Provides links to a variety of topics and programs.

q) **National Association for Home Care and Hospice**
228 7th St. SE, Washington, DC 20003
1-202-547-7424;
www.nahc.org
Gives referrals and offers tips on choosing a homecare agency.

r) **National Pace Association** - 801 N. Fairfax Street, Suite 309, Alexandria, VA 22314; 1-703-535-1566;
www.natlpaceassn.org
Has information on programs and services that provide elderly parents a stay-at-home alternative to nursing home care.

s) **American Association of Homes and Services for the Aging** - 2519 Connecticut Ave., NW, Washington, DC 20008; 1-202-783-2242; *www.aahsa.org* Provides information on housing options, caregiver issues and community services

t) **American Health Care Association & National Center for Assisted Living -** *www.longtermcareliving.com* Helps consumers plan for, cope with and understand option regarding paying for long-term care.

u) **National Academy of Elder Law Attorneys** 1604 N, Country Club Rd., Tucson, AZ 25716 1-520-881-4005; *www.naela.com* Refers site visitors to local elder care attorneys.

v) **Medicare's Nursing Home Compare** - 1-800-633-4227 *www.medicare.gov/NHCompare*

Provides comparative information on nursing homes nationwide including inspection results.

w) **National Caregivers Library -** *www.caregiverslibrary.com* Contains the most comprehensive set of information available to caregivers about seniors' needs and how to meet those needs.

x) **National Adult Day Services Association -** *www.nadsa.org* Provides information on adult daycare centers in your zip code, along with a description of the programs and services offered.

y) **A Place for Mom -** *www.aplaceforMom.com;* 1-800-704-7786 A senior care referral service that helps seniors' families find assisted living facilities, and dementia care for Mom and Dad.

z) **A Consumer Guide to Choosing a Nursing Home** 1-800-633-4277; *www.medicare.gov, www.theconsumervoice.org* or *www.BenefitsCheckUp.org;*

Finds benefit programs that can help seniors pay for medical services, medications, healthcare, food and more.

❖ **Retirement Funding Calculators**:

a) **Edward Jones**: *www.edwardjones.com/retirement*

b) **AARP**: *aarp.org/work/retirement-planning/retirement_calculator*

c) **Charles Schwab**: *www.schwab.com/retirement*

d) **Bankrate**: *www.bankrate.com/calculators/retirement/retirement-plan.com*

e) **CNN Money**: *www.money.cnn.com/calculators/retirement/retirement-need/*

❖ **For Veterans**:

a) *www.military.com/education/gi-bill/guide* Provides information about education benefits for current and former active duty military.

b) **Department of Veterans Affairs** 1-800-827-1000; *www.va.gov*

Provides information to veterans about benefits and eligibility and for referrals to regional offices and VA medical services.

c) **Directory of Veterans Services Organizations, published by the Dept of Veterans Affairs**; *www.va.gov/vso.*

Provides information on vendors providing a wide range of services including education, insurance, home loans extended care, assisted living and health resources.

d) *www.socialworkva.gov/link. asp;* VA social workers advise veterans, their family members, caregivers and friends about getting help from the VA or from community agencies to enable them to continue to live in their own home, and provide help with a variety of programs such as Meals on Wheels.

❖ Volunteering & Learning:

a) Elderhostel - 11 Avenue de Lafayette, Boston, MA 02111 1-877-426-8056; *www.elderhostel.org* Offers educational and travel packages to people 55 and older.

b) Senior Job Bank - *www.seniorjobbank.org* Coordinates seniors wishing to work with potential employers or others looking for volunteers.

c) Senior Service America - 8403 Colesville Rd., Suite 1200, Silver Spring, MD 20910; 1-301-578-8900; *www.seniorserviceamerica.org* Provides job training and placement services to seniors, nationally.

❖ For Kids:

a) *www.kidsenseonline.com*

b) *www.finishrich.com*

c) *www.coolbank.com*

d) *www.kipplinger.com/kids*

e) *www.coolbank.com*

Reverse Mortgages

We've all seen the television ads, often promoted by silver-haired, familiar celebrities who are some of the most well-known actors of our time. Lenders send out colorful brochures promoting their benefits. For homeowners 62 or older with significant equity in their homes, reverse mortgages on their primary residence are described as an easy, simplified way of obtaining money when you most need it, all without having to undergo a credit check. They are described as loans that don't have to be repaid until you die, sell or move out of your house. Those things may be true, but, I encourage you to "look deep before you leap" and educate yourself before using a reverse mortgage as a way of supplementing your income to fill a funding gap.

According to AARP, 600,000 reverse mortgages were issued between 1990 and 2010. The federal Consumer Financial Protection Bureau's statistics show that in 2012, default rates on reverse mortgages were 9.4% - almost double the default rate on conventional mortgages. So, while they were relatively easy to get into, it appears that many reverse mortgage holders were in above their heads and could not continue to meet the program's requirements after the reverse mortgage was granted. The biggest cause of default was non-payment of property taxes and insurance.

Before rushing out to apply for a reverse mortgage, be aware that while this type of loan may provide a ready source of cash, it also has several downsides. Closing costs and fees can be steep, and if you are thinking about moving in two to three years, this may not be the most financially prudent way to extract money from your home. In that case, if there is an urgent cash need, a home equity loan is likely a less costly option.

Following is a summary of what a reverse mortgage is and is not; Federal Housing Authority (FHA) eligibility requirements; repayment requirements and practices; maximum loan amounts; loan disbursement options; a comparison of a home equity loan to a reverse mortgage; and some of the pitfalls of getting one.

What is a reverse mortgage?

Reverse mortgages are pretty complicated financial products. If you're seriously considering one, be sure to talk to a professional (financial planner, tax advisor, attorney) before signing the contract. A reverse mortgage is a special type of loan on a senior homeowner's primary residence that allows the homeowner to convert a part of his/her equity into cash using the home's equity as collateral with no requirement to make monthly payments on the loan. Under the original legislation, governed by the U.S. Department of Housing and Urban Development (HUD), the loan did not to have to be repaid until the last surviving homeowner moved out of the property for more than two years or died. At that time, the estate had only a few months to repay the balance of the reverse mortgage or sell the home. If the home sold for more than the amount due and paid to the mortgage holder, any remaining equity belonged to the estate. If the home sold for less than the balance due on the reverse mortgage, under the laws governing reverse mortgages, the estate was not liable for any shortfall. No other assets of the borrower were affected.

Effective **August 4, 2014**, HUD introduced a new regulation (applicable to FHA-backed reverse mortgages issued on or after that date) that allows the non-borrowing spouse to remain in the home after the borrower dies (and the loan repayment will be deferred), so long as he/she:

- is married to the borrower at the time of the loan closing (and remains married to the borrower for the duration of the borrower's lifetime);
- is named in the loan documents;
- establishes legal ownership (or another ongoing legal right to remain in the home) within 90 days of the death of the last surviving borrower;
- meets all of the obligations described in the loan documents; and

- their spousal status is disclosed at the time of the closing.

If the non-borrowing spouse fails to meet any of the requirements, the loan becomes due and payable. However, if that person re-marries, he/she is no longer eligible for postponement of the repayment of the loan.

Additionally, HUD issued guidance that surviving spouses who were left off a reverse mortgage may receive up to two 60-day extensions delaying the foreclosure once the loan becomes due and payable - one before a foreclosure is started and one during the execution of the foreclosure if the mortgage servicer deems it appropriate.

The new law affects new borrowers only because the old contracts had the old laws embedded in them and HUD felt it had no authority to change those contracts. It expanded the living options for a surviving non-borrowing spouse but left in place the other loan features.

In March, 2014, I encountered an 88-year-old recent widow. She told me there had been a reverse mortgage on their house at the time of her husband's death, but it was in his name only. By law, after he died, his heirs had to pay the bank all of the funds it had advanced him, plus interest, over the years the loan was outstanding. Since she had no funds of her own, this meant she had to either move out of the house so it could be sold to generate the monies owed the bank, borrow the funds from someone so she could pay off the bank but remain in the house, or pray that a fairy godMother would appear and sprinkle down from above the money she needed. (Her income was too low to qualify for a conventional loan.) She ended up moving out of the house she had lived in for 47 years and going to live with one of her grandchildren. The bank sold the property for less than the amount outstanding on the loan, but that was the risk it took. Her deceased husband's heirs did not have to pay the difference. Sadly, within three months, she, too, passed. What had been the family home for almost 50 years also was gone.

Since the new law mentioned above only affects contracts signed after August 4, 2014, the new law would not have helped this widow. But, it will help any of you in her situation with contract dates executed after its enactment.

Before the law changed, the most frequently-used remedy to ensure the surviving spouse was able to remain in the house was to put the reverse mortgage in the names of both spouses, as long as each could qualify individually. With the new law, that is no longer necessary. The non-borrowing, surviving spouse can remain in the house until he/she passes, chooses to move out, or becomes non-compliant.

Who is eligible for a reverse mortgage?

To be eligible for a reverse mortgage, FHA once required that the youngest person whose name is on the title be at least 62 years old. However, that restriction in the law also has changed. Under the new law, a couple now can get a reverse mortgage as long as at least one of the spouses is 62 or older. However, the size of a married couple's payout will be based on the younger spouse's age, even if that spouse isn't on the mortgage title.

The provision in the law remains that the home must be owned free and clear or all existing liens must be satisfied with the proceeds from the reverse mortgage. (If there is an existing mortgage balance, it can be paid off completely with the proceeds of the reverse mortgage loan at closing.) Also, the home still must be the borrower's primary residence.

How does the outstanding amount get repaid?

If the home's equity is higher than the balance of the reverse mortgage loan when the home is sold, the proceeds of the sale are first used to re-pay the loan. Any remaining equity belongs to the estate to do with as it wishes. If the sale of the home is not sufficient to pay off the reverse mortgage, the lender must take a loss and request reimbursement from the FHA.

Is there a maximum amount for a reverse mortgage loan?

The maximum loan amount generally depends on the following four factors:

1. The borrower's age
2. Then-current interest rates
3. The home's appraised value
4. Then-current government-imposed lending limits.

In most cases, the more valuable the home, the higher the loan amount, subject to FHA lending limits.

How is the money from a reverse mortgage paid out?

There are at least five ways the proceeds of a reverse mortgage can be distributed. These include:

1. A lump sum of cash given the borrower at closing
2. Monthly payments as long as he/she lives in the home
3. Equal monthly payments for a fixed number of years
4. A line of credit which allows the homeowner to draw any amount at any time until the line of credit is exhausted

5.   A combination of the ways listed above.

Be sure to choose the option that works best for your situation. If you know someone who has taken out a reverse mortgage, don't automatically take the same option he/she took. Evaluate your own needs and take the one that serves you best. For example, if your monthly income is not enough for you to comfortably pay your utilities, buy your medicine and pay for your food, then either Option 2 or Option 3 may be best because each allows you to receive monthly payments as an addition to your limited monthly income. On the other hand, if your aging home needs major repairs, like a new roof, a one-time cash infusion such as the lump sum offered in Option 1 might be preferred.

How does a reverse mortgage differ from a home equity loan?

Generally speaking, a home equity loan or a home equity line of credit (commonly referred to as a HELOC) has very strict income and creditworthiness requirements. In the case of a HELOC, once it is granted, the homeowner must make monthly payments to repay the outstanding loan. A reverse mortgage loan has no creditworthiness requirements, but, effective January 1, 2015, the bank will be required to perform the financial assessment described in #3 below. Also, with a reverse mortgage, instead of making monthly mortgage payments **to** the lender, the homeowner receives cash **from** the lender. The loan typically is not due as long as the mortgage holder (or spouse) lives in the home as his/her primary residence and continues to meet all loan obligations and requirements.

What are some pitfalls of a reverse mortgage?

In July, 2014, the new Reverse Mortgage Stabilization Act was signed into law and several new reverse mortgage rules were enacted. These new rules were designed to stabilize the program, minimize risk and reduce the default rate. Following is a summary of the five new rules contained in the act.

1. **You might receive less cash than under the old program**. Under a new rule, effective September 30, 2014, the FHA cut by 15% the percent of equity you can remove from your home through a reverse mortgage.

2. **The amount of upfront cash you may receive is limited**. The new rule limits to 60% the amount of cash you may withdraw during the first 12 months of loan approval. An exception may be made to cover "mandatory obligations" such as an existing mortgage and delinquent federal debts.

3. **You might not qualify**. While there is no minimum credit score requirement, effective January 1, 2015, borrowers must undergo a financial assessment to qualify for a reverse mortgage. This includes an analysis of mortgage debt(s), credit card and other payment histories, and confirmation of up-to-date insurance policies. The analysis also checks for unpaid liens against the property and delinquent debts owed to the federal government.

4. **You may have to pay more in fees.** Fees now are based on the amount of equity a homeowner withdraws. Borrowers who withdraw more than 60% of their equity in the first year of the loan will pay an upfront mortgage insurance premium equal to 2.5% of the appraised value of their home. At only 0.5%, the premium is substantially lower for borrowers who withdraw less than 60% of their available equity in the first year. (Previous fees were between 0.01% and 2.0%). Borrowers must continue to pay an annual mortgage insurance premium which remains at 1.25% of the loan balance.

5. **You may be required to set up an escrow account to cover property taxes**. To reduce default rates by ensuring borrowers have the funds to cover property taxes and insurance, some borrowers will be required to set aside additional cash (similar to an escrow account) as part of a new rule that goes into effect January 1, 2015. A single

homeowner with at least $529 remaining each month after paying his/her expenses likely will not be required to set aside funds for property taxes and insurance, according to a HUD letter sent to borrowers. (Couples and families will have to show additional income to avoid the set-aside requirement.)

Borrowers who don't meet the minimum income requirements either will be required to set aside funds to cover property taxes and homeowners insurance for the life of the loan, called a Lifetime Expectancy Set Aside, or have these fees withdrawn from monthly reverse mortgage payments they receive.

Here are a few other reasons to think twice about getting a reverse mortgage:

1. **The basic fees are often high**. Since a reverse mortgage is a loan, there will be loan-related fees. Origination fees and other fees on a reverse mortgage are usually rather high. Because a reverse mortgage is a home equity loan that isn't decided based solely on your income or credit score, there are unique risks to the lender. Some of those risks often are offset by charging higher loan fees. These fees are in addition to the mortgage insurance premium described above.

2. **The interest rate is often higher than typical market rates.** The interest rate on a reverse mortgage is often higher than the rate for a more traditional home equity loan. Between the up-front fees on the reverse mortgage and the high interest charges, you might be surprised at how little money you actually end up netting.

3. **Your heirs might not get the house**. As mentioned above, when you get a reverse mortgage, you aren't required to make payments on the loan. Instead, the loan is paid off when the home is sold. So, if you die, the home is expected to be sold (unless you have a surviving spouse who lives in the house), hopefully, at an amount that will cover the loan

balance. Your heirs don't automatically get the house unless they pay off the reverse mortgage. However, this usually means that the money has to come out of the estate, reducing the total your heirs end up with. For someone hoping to leave a significant legacy, this could be a real drawback. If the heirs do not choose to pay off then loan, then the house becomes the property of the bank.

4. **You may have to repay the loan if and when you move out**. Dying isn't the only way repayment of a reverse mortgage is triggered. In order to avoid making payments on the loan, you have to be living most of the time in the home as your primary residence. (You are considered "moved out" if you haven't lived in the home for a year. This includes if you enter a long-term-care facility.) So, if you are no longer able to stay in your home, you may have to start repaying your reverse mortgage at a time when money is likely already tight. This can put a real strain on your budget.

5. **You're still responsible for the costs associated with maintaining your home**. Throughout all of this, you are still responsible for all of the expenses associated with your home. You have to pay property taxes; stay current on your homeowners insurance; pay HOA fees; and pay for regular maintenance of the home. If you have enough equity, you may be able to get a reverse mortgage big enough to cover all these expenses, but, it can be a difficult situation nonetheless.

Before deciding to get a reverse mortgage, carefully think through the situation. The high costs, combined with the difficulties that can arise if you want to move out of the house or leave property to your heirs, can make a reverse mortgage more trouble than it's worth. A better solution, if you're strapped for funds, may be to look for creative ways to help you generate the cash needed without the baggage of a reverse mortgage. In the end, the choice is yours.

Appendix F

More of Mimi's Favorite Sayings

1. A scared man can't gamble and a jealous man can't sleep.
2. A sleeping man is a dead man.
3. It's always darkest before the dawn.
4. Don't rain on my parade.
5. The sun's gonna shine in my backyard someday.
6. There is none so blind as he who will not see.
7. You can lead a horse to water, but you can't make him drink it.
8. You can pick your friends, but you can't pick your relatives.
9. Don't blame the messenger for the message.
10. Even a fish wouldn't get caught if he kept his mouth shut.
11. Better to close your mouth and be thought a fool than to open it and remove all doubt.
12. If the Lord had wanted me to fly, he'd have given me wings. (on her fear of flying)
13. An apple never falls far from the tree.
14. A leopard doesn't change its spots.
15. Nothing spoils a duck but his bill.
16. A cow needs its tail more than one fly season.
17. Why buy the cow if the milk is free?
18. If the Lord had wanted me to work that hard, he'd have made me a mule.
19. A man can't ride your back unless it's bent.
20. Don't do as I do; do as I say do.
21. Two heads are better than one. (on collaborating)
22. Time waits for no man.
23. What Mother Nature doesn't cure, Father Time will.
24. A dog that brings a bone will carry a bone.
25. Options are for today's parents. When I was raising children, I knew what I was doing. I didn't need your help!

Index

About the Author

Patricia Davis is a former corporate financial management executive. She has held significant financial management positions with some of the nation's premier organizations such as Transamerica, Bank of America, WorldCom and the Federal Reserve Board. Today, she uses her extensive financial expertise to conduct seminars, nationwide, on Financial Literacy and to provide personal financial counseling to individuals (and couples) at all income levels, but with a special emphasis on under-served populations. Mrs. Davis is the Managing Director of Davis Financial Services and is the Executive Director of Money Matters, Inc., a 501C (3) non-profit corporation. Both provide financial literacy education and training, and financial counseling. Also, she is a licensed provider of Camp Millionaire, a financial literacy education program for kids, teens and adults.

Mrs. Davis, a native Washingtonian, graduated with honors from Howard University with a B.S. in mathematics and statistics; and finished near the top of her M.B.A. class at Stanford University's Graduate School of Business. She has an M.S. in Personal Financial Planning from Golden Gate University where she received her class' Top Student Award. Also, she graduated with distinction from the Stonier Graduate School of Banking at Georgetown University.

Mrs. Davis is a former White House Fellow and served as Special Assistant to the Secretary of Labor. In 2009, she was appointed one of her state's two representatives to the Internal Revenue Service's Taxpayer Advocacy Panel, a citizen's advocacy group that focuses on improving IRS responsiveness to taxpayer needs. She has been awarded Golden Gate University's Alumni Community Service Award in acknowledgement of her work providing financial literacy to under-served populations.

Mrs. Davis is the author of the financial management primer, *Mimi, Money and Me 101 Realities About Money Daddy Never Taught Me but Mama Always Knew*. The book has been endorsed by the Washington Post's financial columnist, Michelle Singletary, as "... one of the best books to give if you want to give the gift of financial power."

Mrs. Davis is a marathoner; is married; and travels extensively.

CPSIA information can be obtained
at www.ICGtesting.com
Printed in the USA
FFOW05n1727240615